My Asia Geography Factbook

A Workbook that encompasses the entire continent of Asia.

By Brandy Champeau

Exploring Expression

ISBN-13: 978-1-954057-03-6

A note about this Factbook

The Asia Geography Factbook is a workbook. While there are a number of YouTube videos listed *(and I encourage you to watch them all)* it is **up to you, the learner**, to complete the pages and build your factbook. This means that you may want to (or need to) do a bit of research to find some of the answers within.

This also means that while many of the aspects will be similar, your finished product will not necessarily look like your neighbors.

Your ***My Asia Geography Factbook*** will be what **you** make it – a comprehensive keepsake guide created by you as you learn about all of the wonderful countries that make up the continent of Asia.

Happy Learning!!

Brandy Champeau, CEO

Exploring Expression, LLC

https://ExploringExpression.com

Asia

Books about Asia

1.   (Y, O) ***Draw Asia: Volume 1 & 2*** by Kristin J. Draeger

2.   (Y) ***Asia (A True Book: Geography: Continents)*** by John Son

3.   (O) ***A Short History of Asia*** by Colin Mason

4.   (Y) ***Explore Asia (Explore the Continents)*** by Bobbie Kalman and Rebecca Sjonger

5.   (O) ***Asia Beyond Growth: Urbanization in the World's Fastest-changing Continent*** by AECOM

6.   (O) ***Restless Continent: Wealth, Rivalry and Asia's New Geopolitics*** by Michael Wesley

7.   (O) ***When Asia Was the World: Traveling Merchants, Scholars, Warriors, and Monks Who Created the "Riches of the ""East"*** by Stewart Gordon

Games about Asia

1.   Ticket to Ride: Asia Map Collection One

2.   World Card Series Asia Continent Deck - Geography Playing Card Game

3.   GeoToys — GeoPuzzle Asia

4.   10 Days in Asia

* (O) books are for older readers; (Y) books are for younger readers

Movies about Asia

1. Aladdin animated (1992)(G)
2. Aladdin live action (2019)(PG)
3. Mulan animated (1998)(G)
4. Mulan Live action (2020)(PG-13)
5. The jungle book animated (1967)(G)
6. The Jungle Book live action (2016)(PG)
7. Eat, Pray Love (2010)(PG-13)
8. Lara Croft: Tomb Raider (2001)(PG-13)
9. Kong: Skull Island (2017)(PG-13)
10. The Impossible (2012)(PG-13)
11. The Bridge on the river Kwai (1957)(PG)
12. The Birth of Sake (2016)(NR)
13. The Propaganda Game (2015)(NR)
14. They call it Myanmar – Lifting the Curtain (2012)(NR)
15. The Karate Kid (2010)(PG)
16. Kung Foo Panda (2008)(PG)

YouTube videos about Asia General

- Asia/Continent of Asia/Asia Geography
  - https://www.youtube.com/watch?v=exeKgohZWRo
- A Tour of Southeast Asia - Full Documentary
  - https://www.youtube.com/watch?v=WnnFMv9GCH4
- Asian History Documentary
  - https://www.youtube.com/watch?v=FPaPD-atXe4
- Asia | Destination World
  - https://www.youtube.com/watch?v=nsOtOye-DJM
- Map of Asia Continent (Countries and their location)
  - https://www.youtube.com/watch?v=Sns7EOIgMzU
- Where Are The Asian Borders? (part 1)
  - https://www.youtube.com/watch?v=vPupwlZlNMY
- Why Do India And China Have So Many People?
  - https://www.youtube.com/watch?v=V7oiro8tYA4
- Deserts in Asia – Destroyers of Civilization Pt. 1 | Full Documentary
  - https://www.youtube.com/watch?v=pw6k0QBTYb4
- World Geography - The Geography of Asia and the Pacific
  - https://www.youtube.com/watch?v=x-LFOkGfyZM

Continent Fact File: Asia

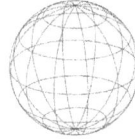

Hemisphere
(circle one)

Population:_____

Area: _____

Highest Point: _____

Longest River: _____

Tallest Waterfall: _____

Number of countries:

_____

Largest Country: _____

Northern

Southern

Both

Major
Biomes

1:_____

2: _____

3: _____

 Other Cool Things about this Continent

1:_____

2: _____

3: _____

4: _____

Map it Out: Asia

Color and Label the following on the map of Africa:

- ❏ Pacific Ocean,
- ❏ Indian Ocean,
- ❏ Arctic Ocean,
- ❏ Arabian Sea,
- ❏ Bay of Bengal,

- ❏ South China Sea,
- ❏ Yellow Sea,
- ❏ Bering Sea
- ❏ Himalayas,
- ❏ Ural Mountains

- ❏ Mount Everest,
- ❏ Siberia
- ❏ Arabian Desert,
- ❏ Gobi Desert

World Wonders in Asia

Wonders of the World in Asia

Wonders of the ancient World

- **Hanging gardens of Babylon (Iraq)**
  - Hanging Gardens of Babylon - The Seven Wonders of the Ancient World - See U in History
    - https://www.youtube.com/watch?v=DmglKtom7YE
  - Secrets Of Ancient Hanging Gardens of Babylon Ancient Mysteries Documentary
    - https://www.youtube.com/watch?v=LEjIdn_4aTY
  - Who Built The Hanging Gardens of Babylon? | Secrets of The Dead | PBS
    - https://www.youtube.com/watch?v=F6vVxbAJAog

- **Statue of Zeus at Olympia (Greece)**
  - The Temple of Zeus in Olimpia - The Seven Wonders of the Ancient World - See U in History
    - https://www.youtube.com/watch?v=7lDW7jrDfRY&t=1s
  - Great Wonders: The Statue of Zeus at Olympia
    - https://www.youtube.com/watch?v=9ngny7zfrTU
  - Ancient Greece - Statue of Olympian Zeus
    - https://www.youtube.com/watch?v=Q9T9ar6K-No

- **Temple of Artemis at Ephesus (Turkey)**
  - The Temple of Artemis in Ephesus - 7 Wonder of the Ancient World - See U in History
    - https://www.youtube.com/watch?v=Qr3nBLnj-8E
  - Learning-History: The Temple of Artemis
    - https://www.youtube.com/watch?v=Cf6t1b_T6FI
  - Why was the Temple of Artemis one of the Wonders of the Ancient World?
    - https://www.youtube.com/watch?v=7SD0uwldOPE

Wonders of the World in Asia

Wonders of the ancient World

- **Mausoleum at Halicarnassus (Turkey)**
    - Mausoleum at Halicarnassus - 7 Wonders of the Ancient World - See U in History
        - https://www.youtube.com/watch?v=fQwCwcvlp-Y
    - Great Wonders: The Mausoleum of Halicarnassus and its Successors
        - https://www.youtube.com/watch?v=6F-iKIz6b8Q
    - The Mausoleum at Halicarnassus: 7 Ancient Wonders
        - https://www.youtube.com/watch?v=xhVP4OQrTzE

- **Colossus of Rhodes (Greece)**
    - The Colossus of Rhodes - 7 Wonders of the Ancient World - See U in History
        - https://www.youtube.com/watch?v=MbFayW5xB9s
    - The Seven Wonders of the Ancient World Episode 2: The Colossus of Rhodes
        - https://www.youtube.com/watch?v=hh-x-KEo4Tg
    - The Colossus of Rhodes: 7 Ancient Wonders
        - https://www.youtube.com/watch?v=vJnEdUrWNsU

Wonders of the World in Asia

Wonders of the natural world

- **Mount Everest (Nepal/china)**
  - Mount Everest: The Tallest Mountain on Earth | How the Earth Was Made | Full Documentary | History
    - https://www.youtube.com/watch?v=3-oYON9V8tA
  - Why is Mount Everest so tall? - Michele Koppes
    - https://www.youtube.com/watch?v=uy9GFAOGGXU
  - What Happens to Your Body When You Climb Everest
    - https://www.youtube.com/watch?v=ZXI7Mxv0WDU

- **Aurora Borealis (Russia)**
  - Aurora Borealis in Murmansk, Russia, November 2017
    - https://www.youtube.com/watch?v=WWhdF9Jy9Lo
  - Discovering Russia: Polar Nights & Northern Lights (RT Documentary)
    - https://www.youtube.com/watch?v=bqn6yKtFvIU

Wonders of the World in Asia

New wonders of the world

- **Great wall of china (China)**
  - National Geographic - The Great Wall of China - Documentary
    - https://www.youtube.com/watch?v=VjlydnRqcmw
  - What makes the Great Wall of China so extraordinary - Megan Campisi and Pen-Pen Chen
    - https://www.youtube.com/watch?v=23oHqNEqRyo
  - How and Why the Great Wall of China Was Really Built
    - https://www.youtube.com/watch?v=m68zyXyeYG0

- **Petra (Jordan)**
  - Petra, Jordan | Civilisations - BBC Two
    - https://www.youtube.com/watch?v=SZ5JjLdzQ1o
  - Stunning Stone Monuments of Petra | National Geographic
    - https://www.youtube.com/watch?v=ezDiSkOU0wc
  - The Lost City of Petra Documentary 2017
    - https://www.youtube.com/watch?v=6kKjARnkbtA

- **Taj Mahal (India)**
  - Lost Worlds: Taj Mahal (S2, E18) | Full Episode | History
    - https://www.youtube.com/watch?v=4uszZG0x2Gk
  - The Story of the Taj Mahal for Kids: Famous World Landmarks for Children - FreeSchool
    - https://www.youtube.com/watch?v=I6i8cLXPGQE
  - Taj Mahal: How the Most Beautiful Building in the World Came to Be
    - https://www.youtube.com/watch?v=6tsHnxoboN4

Wonders of the World: Hanging Gardens of Babylon

Draw a Picture of the wonder.

Mark the Location on the Map of Asia

This is a (circle one):	Original Wonder of the World	New Wonder of the World	Wonder of the Natural World

Write a description of the wonder:

Why is it considered a wonder of the world?

Wonders of the World: Statue of Zeus at Olympia

Draw a Picture of the wonder.

Mark the Location on the Map of Asia

This is a (circle one):	Original Wonder of the World	New Wonder of the World	Wonder of the Natural World

Write a description of the wonder:

Why is it considered a wonder of the world?

Wonders of the World: Temple of Artemis at Ephesus

Draw a Picture of the wonder.

Mark the Location on the Map of Asia

This is a (circle one):	Original Wonder of the World	New Wonder of the World	Wonder of the Natural World

Write a description of the wonder:

Why is it considered a wonder of the world?

Wonders of the World: Mausoleum at Halicarnassus

Draw a Picture of the wonder.

Mark the Location on the Map of Asia

| This is a (circle one): | Original Wonder of the World | New Wonder of the World | Wonder of the Natural World |

Write a description of the wonder:

Why is it considered a wonder of the world?

Wonders of the World: Colossus of Rhodes

Draw a Picture of the wonder.

Mark the Location on the Map of Asia

This is a (circle one):	Original Wonder of the World	New Wonder of the World	Wonder of the Natural World

Write a description of the wonder:

Why is it considered a wonder of the world?

Wonders of the World: Mount Everest

Draw a Picture of the wonder.

Mark the Location on the Map of Asia

This is a (circle one):	Original Wonder of the World	New Wonder of the World	Wonder of the Natural World

Write a description of the wonder:

Why is it considered a wonder of the world?

Wonders of the World: Aurora Borealis

Draw a Picture of the wonder.

Mark the Location on the Map of Asia

This is a (circle one): | Original Wonder of the World | New Wonder of the World | Wonder of the Natural World

Write a description of the wonder:

Why is it considered a wonder of the world?

Wonders of the World: Great Wall of China

Draw a Picture of the wonder.

Mark the Location on the Map of Asia

| This is a (circle one): | Original Wonder of the World | New Wonder of the World | Wonder of the Natural World |

Write a description of the wonder:

Why is it considered a wonder of the world?

Wonders of the World: Petra

Draw a Picture of the wonder.

Mark the Location on the Map of Asia

This is a (circle one):	Original Wonder of the World	New Wonder of the World	Wonder of the Natural World

Write a description of the wonder:

Why is it considered a wonder of the world?

Wonders of the World: Taj Mahal

Draw a Picture of the wonder.

Mark the Location on the Map of Asia

This is a (circle one):	Original Wonder of the World	New Wonder of the World	Wonder of the Natural World

Write a description of the wonder:

Why is it considered a wonder of the world?

Countries of Asia
Videos

Countries of Asia

1. Afghanistan
2. Armenia
3. Azerbaijan
4. Bahrain
5. Bangladesh
6. Bhutan
7. Brunei
8. Cambodia
9. China
10. Cyprus
11. Georgia
12. India
13. Indonesia
14. Iran
15. Iraq
16. Israel
17. Japan
18. Jordan
19. Kazakhstan
20. Kuwait
21. Kyrgyzstan
22. Laos
23. Lebanon
24. Malaysia
25. Maldives
26. Mongolia
27. Myanmar
28. Nepal
29. North Korea
30. Oman
31. Pakistan
32. Palestine State
33. Philippines
34. Qatar
35. Russia
36. Saudi Arabia
37. Singapore
38. South Korea
39. Sri Lanka
40. Syria
41. Taiwan
42. Tajikistan
43. Thailand
44. Timor-Leste
45. Turkey
46. Turkmenistan
47. United Arab Emirates
48. Uzbekistan
49. Vietnam
50. Yemen

Countries of Asia

Afghanistan

- Geography Now! Afghanistan
  - https://www.youtube.com/watch?v=ipVw772hCrM
- Afghanistan | Wild Shepherdess with Kate Humble | BBC Documentary
  - https://www.youtube.com/watch?v=UP8pA0v6QFE

Armenia

- Geography Now! Armenia
  - https://www.youtube.com/watch?v=sL4JK_bDo0A
- The history of Armenia Summarized
  - https://www.youtube.com/watch?v=aT9A_nCuU-Q

Azerbaijan

- Geography Now! Azerbaijan
  - https://www.youtube.com/watch?v=DqVPVRmRIU8
- Things worth knowing about Azerbaijan
  - https://www.youtube.com/watch?v=qlv5N9helDo

Bahrain

- Geography Now! Bahrain
  - https://www.youtube.com/watch?v=P2gHUcwZbYk
- 15 Things You Didn't Know About BAHRAIN
  - https://www.youtube.com/watch?v=2ITpD4vfRzM

Bangladesh

- Geography Now! Bangladesh
  - https://www.youtube.com/watch?v=Ijebhxk_9ys
- 15 Things You Didn't Know About Bangladesh
  - https://www.youtube.com/watch?v=XvQmFpwQILE

Bhutan

- Geography Now! Bhutan
  - https://www.youtube.com/watch?v=v3_EezKE0WI
- 10 Surprising Facts About Bhutan
  - https://www.youtube.com/watch?v=Vw758WFuitw

Countries of Asia

Brunei

- Geography Now! Brunei
  - https://www.youtube.com/watch?v=bNTTFmgbPZY
- The Richest Country You've Never Heard Of
  - https://www.youtube.com/watch?v=PLv9I9YviSc
- Cambodia
  - Geography Now! Cambodia
    - https://www.youtube.com/watch?v=wufWxldBWsU
  - CAMBODIA Top 10 Things You NEED to Know
    - https://www.youtube.com/watch?v=I16dr1YfGLQ

China

- Geography Now! China
  - https://www.youtube.com/watch?v=IzAESaVqix0
- 15 Things You Didn't Know About China
  - https://www.youtube.com/watch?v=aMXQMFCh9xY
- All China's dynasties explained in 7 minutes (5,000 years of Chinese history)
  - https://www.youtube.com/watch?v=fFNzX3tYTXU

Cyprus

- Geography Now! Cyprus
  - https://www.youtube.com/watch?v=4w_Vc_7irhM
- 15 Things You Didn't Know About Cyprus
  - https://www.youtube.com/watch?v=4ehCCjeUIQ0

Georgia

- Geography Now! Georgia
  - https://www.youtube.com/watch?v=YWXvDxovfM4
- Why Is Georgia The Name Of A Country & State?
  - https://www.youtube.com/watch?v=0qinN4NtW-I

India

- Geography Now! India
  - https://www.youtube.com/watch?v=vEy6tcU6eLU
- The States + territories of India EXPLAINED Geography Now!
  - https://www.youtube.com/watch?v=8RhRokdQtoo

Countries of Asia

Indonesia

- Geography Now! Indonesia
  - https://www.youtube.com/watch?v=FsXc3FcWi3g
- Flag/ fan Friday! INDONESIA (Geography Now!)
  - https://www.youtube.com/watch?v=SDD0r15AprU

Iran

- Geography Now! Iran
  - https://www.youtube.com/watch?v=2xQM4Zy5zIk&t=1s
- Flag/ Fan Friday! IRAN (Geography Now!)
  - https://www.youtube.com/watch?v=AuNgViDeXF0

Iraq

- Geography Now! IRAQ
  - https://www.youtube.com/watch?v=YHQqsx9wsnc&t=6s
- Flag / Fan Friday IRAQ (Geography Now!)
  - https://www.youtube.com/watch?v=pFtKaT3GF9I

Israel

- Geography Now! ISRAEL
  - https://www.youtube.com/watch?v=AWKmazrRIwA
- Flag/ Fan Friday! Israel
  - https://www.youtube.com/watch?v=g-Ie90ejFjs

Japan

- Geography Now! Japan
  - https://www.youtube.com/watch?v=j3XpfBChLyk&t=232s
- Flag/ Fan SUNDAY, Japan! (Geography Now)
  - https://www.youtube.com/watch?v=t1nhAnMQBHg&t=1s
- History of Japan Documentary
  - https://www.youtube.com/watch?v=JCBFomgHoFA

Jordan

- Geography Now! Jordan
  - https://www.youtube.com/watch?v=aWfu0BKOZ5g
- Flag / Fan Friday JORDAN (Geography Now!)
  - https://www.youtube.com/watch?v=YCy7QYzGTj4

Countries of Asia

Kazakhstan

- Geography Now! Kazakhstan
    - https://www.youtube.com/watch?v=BEIOyEjTujk
- Flag/ Fan Friday, KAZAKHSTAN (Geography Now!)
    - https://www.youtube.com/watch?v=9Zv2CX93_xs

Kuwait

- Geography Now! KUWAIT
    - https://www.youtube.com/watch?v=S_pUIeE4Eko
- FLAG/ FAN FRIDAY KUWAIT, Got something from ANTARCTICA! (Geography Now!
    - https://www.youtube.com/watch?v=JgdYMPkFNyM

Kyrgyzstan

- Geography Now! Kyrgyzstan
    - https://www.youtube.com/watch?v=Wo-b_MpguLo
- Flag / Fan Friday KYRGYZSTAN! (Geography Now!)
    - https://www.youtube.com/watch?v=Uin3RonY0Hw

Laos

- Geography Now! LAOS
    - https://www.youtube.com/watch?v=dbmZQDySpzY
- Flag/ Fan Friday LAOS (Geography Now!)
    - https://www.youtube.com/watch?v=5ctnnSJWjkc

Lebanon

- Geography Now! LEBANON
    - https://www.youtube.com/watch?v=vvgLLqpRT6s
- Flag/ Fan Friday LEBANON (Geography Now!)
    - https://www.youtube.com/watch?v=0t-UiVWYKQA

Malaysia

- Geography Now! MALAYSIA
    - https://www.youtube.com/watch?v=dV-H1EKmCxA
- Flag/ Fan Friday MALAYSIA! (Geography Now!)
    - https://www.youtube.com/watch?v=PfpwNYNeztU

Countries of Asia

Maldives

- Geography Now! MALDIVES
    - https://www.youtube.com/watch?v=KzuWHTJWe-0
- Flag / Fan Friday MALDIVES! (Geography Now!)
    - https://www.youtube.com/watch?v=0YH1XuEnXGo

Mongolia

- Geography Now! MONGOLIA
    - https://www.youtube.com/watch?v=TpdGIPHPBwU
- Flag / Fan Friday MONGOLIA Geography Now
    - https://www.youtube.com/watch?v=ZbH7LboqTxQ

Myanmar

- Geography Now! MYANMAR
    - https://www.youtube.com/watch?v=xMaaUTWzv8U
- Flag/ Fan Friday MYANMAR (Geography Now!)
    - https://www.youtube.com/watch?v=7jwBS0TBTuQ

Nepal

- Geography Now! NEPAL
    - https://www.youtube.com/watch?v=8gTkgfOMkTU
- Flag / Fan Friday NEPAL (Geography Now!)
    - https://www.youtube.com/watch?v=KSMMWzRomhI

North Korea

- Geography Now! North Korea (DPRK)
    - https://www.youtube.com/watch?v=00QUYoZHnH8
- Flag/ Fan Friday NORTH KOREA (Geography Now!)
    - https://www.youtube.com/watch?v=oiL0u00nMzI

Countries of Asia

Oman

- Geography Now! OMAN
    - https://www.youtube.com/watch?v=mw-gmjzN4Fw
- Flag/ Fan Friday OMAN (Geography Now!)
    - https://www.youtube.com/watch?v=3cAmGRX5XEg

Pakistan

- Geography Now! PAKISTAN
    - https://www.youtube.com/watch?v=CqP2fiqlVok
- Flag/ Fan Friday PAKISTAN (Geography Now!)
    - https://www.youtube.com/watch?v=WAbsXBv9zvs

Palestine State

- Palestine geography
    - https://www.youtube.com/watch?v=rYFVX0YBJIY
- Why Isn't Palestine A State Yet?
    - https://www.youtube.com/watch?v=Dyqx7CDGrTA

Philippines

- Geography Now! Philippines
    - https://www.youtube.com/watch?v=LVFvRNRTEd4
- THE HISTORY OF THE PHILIPPINES in 12 minutes
    - https://www.youtube.com/watch?v=P-I4Bay5SXo

Qatar

- Geography Now! QATAR
    - https://www.youtube.com/watch?v=oqfW7xn215o&t=602s
- Flag/ Fan Friday QATAR (Geography Now!)
    - https://www.youtube.com/watch?v=iK2gSBrSRWk

Countries of Asia

Russia

- Geography Now! RUSSIA
  - https://www.youtube.com/watch?v=K8zAbdYx9SU&t=1476s
- Flag/ Fan Friday RUSSIA (Geography Now!)
  - https://www.youtube.com/watch?v=yM6QQvkpJtY
- History of Russia in 10 Minutes | The Animated Russian History in a Nutshell
  - https://www.youtube.com/watch?v=LYrGnPvWTvQ

Saudi Arabia

- Geography Now! SAUDI ARABIA
  - https://www.youtube.com/watch?v=tP68QwVvAZk
- FLAG/ FAN FRIDAY SAUDI ARABIA! (Geography Now)
  - https://www.youtube.com/watch?v=wC90N9AcPLU

Singapore

- Geography Now! SINGAPORE
  - https://www.youtube.com/watch?v=w-z4q7F5Bcs
- FLAG/ FAN FRIDAY SINGAPORE! (Geography Now!)
  - https://www.youtube.com/watch?v=9_Ra0wqWeWQ

South Korea

- Geography Now! SOUTH KOREA (ROK)
  - https://www.youtube.com/watch?v=zTK119W8MBA
- Flag/ Fan Friday SOUTH KOREA (Geography Now!)
  - https://www.youtube.com/watch?v=HYvM-zEBkHA

Sri Lanka

- Zooming in on SRI LANKA | Geography of Sri Lanka with Google Earth
  - https://www.youtube.com/watch?v=8V2LJ726F4s
- Why Has Sri Lanka Had So Many Names?
  - https://www.youtube.com/watch?v=U14z2Tr_ZpE

Countries of Asia

Syria

- Syria Geography/Syria Country/Syria
  - https://www.youtube.com/watch?v=smy-XARszxg
- Syria Geography
  - https://www.youtube.com/watch?v=MxVVGwN1vYw
- The war in Syria explained in five minutes | Guardian Animations
  - https://www.youtube.com/watch?v=K5H5w3_QTG0

Taiwan

- 15 Things You Didn't Know About Taiwan
  - https://www.youtube.com/watch?v=5lj4hLZER1c
- Is Taiwan a country... or part of China?
  - https://www.youtube.com/watch?v=KQTtwh2GRME

Tajikistan

- Zooming in on TAJIKISTAN | Geography of Tajikistan with Google Earth
  - https://www.youtube.com/watch?v=jFhgbluits8
- A lesser known Asian country: Tajikistan
  - https://www.youtube.com/watch?v=Eb6OxDGaEmo

Thailand

- Focus on Thailand! Country Profile and Geographical Info
  - https://www.youtube.com/watch?v=6riSxKo3obg
- The History of Thailand Explained in 5 minutes
  - https://www.youtube.com/watch?v=OfOMEP_7AJM

Countries of Asia

Timor-Leste

- Geography Now! East Timor
  - https://www.youtube.com/watch?v=Yy2OZZJwBYU
- Geography Now! EAST TIMOR (Flag Friday)
  - https://www.youtube.com/watch?v=taTZT9aHLVQ

Turkey

- Zooming in on Turkey | Geography of Turkey with Google Earth
  - https://www.youtube.com/watch?v=A44bVaeFJhk
- THE HISTORY OF TURKEY in 10 minutes
  - https://www.youtube.com/watch?v=sp8J4za_3GI

Turkmenistan

- Zooming in on TURKMENISTAN | Geography of Turkmenistan with Google Earth
  - https://www.youtube.com/watch?v=yWqtldbO4Lc
- Undercover in Turkmenistan | Full Documentary | TRACKS
  - https://www.youtube.com/watch?v=wmyNAcKcWa8

United Arab Emirates

- UAE Explained
  - https://www.youtube.com/watch?v=aNczga-dw0I
- Zooming in on United Arab Emirates | Geography of United Arab Emirates
  - https://www.youtube.com/watch?v=j3ZcBhLpdO8

Countries of Asia

Uzbekistan

- Zooming in on Uzbekistan | Geography of Uzbekistan with Google Earth
  - https://www.youtube.com/watch?v=O0KwS4mpXJg
- The people, history and culture of Uzbekistan - Traveling the Silk Road | DW Documentary
  - https://www.youtube.com/watch?v=KoH2bU9xADg

Vietnam

- History of Vietnam explained in 8 minutes (All Vietnamese dynasties)
  - https://www.youtube.com/watch?v=u8R9MtM42P8
- Geopolitics of Vietnam
  - https://www.youtube.com/watch?v=Z5Mr7ssxC60

Yemen

- Zooming in on YEMEN | Geography of Yemen with Google Earth
  - https://www.youtube.com/watch?v=TzI5sSv1kFU
- Things you didn't know about Yemen
  - https://www.youtube.com/watch?v=tgZrRkbmDXQ
- History of Yemen
  - https://www.youtube.com/watch?v=jtHCzp2r9So

Countries of Asia
Worksheets

Afghanistan

Color the country's flag in the box above.

Label the capital city and any major physical features such as mountains, rivers, oceans or seas **in or around** this country.

Country Name: Afghanistan

FACTS

Population:_____

Area: _____

Type of Government: _____

Capital City: _____

Religion(s): _____

Language(s): _____

Currency: _____

Climate: _____

Time Zone: _____

Major Exports

1:_____

2:_____

3:_____

Mountains, Rivers and Lakes

1:_____

2:_____

3:_____

Other Cool Things about this Country

1:_____

2:_____

3:_____

4:_____

Armenia

Color the country's flag in the box above.

Label the capital city and any major physical features such as mountains, rivers, oceans or seas **in or around** this country.

Country Name: Armenia

FACTS

Population:_____

Area: _____

Type of Government: _____

Capital City: _____

Religion(s): _____

Language(s): _____

Currency: _____

Climate: _____

Time Zone: _____

Major Exports

1:_____

2: _____

3: _____

Mountains, Rivers and Lakes

1:_____

2: _____

3: _____

Other Cool Things about this Country

1:_____

2: _____

3: _____

4: _____

Azerbaijan

Color the country's flag in the box above.

Label the capital city and any major physical features such as mountains, rivers, oceans or seas **in or around** this country.

Country Name: Azerbaijan

FACTS

Population:_____

Area: _____

Type of Government: _____

Capital City: _____

Religion(s): _____

Language(s): _____

Currency: _____

Climate: _____

Time Zone: _____

Major Exports

1:_____

2: _____

3: _____

Mountains, Rivers and Lakes

1:_____

2: _____

3: _____

Other Cool Things about this Country

1:_____

2: _____

3: _____

4: _____

Bahrain

Color the country's flag in the box above.

Label the capital city and any major physical features such as mountains, rivers, oceans or seas **in or around** this country.

Country Name: Bahrain

FACTS

Population:_____

Area: _____

Type of Government: _____

Capital City: _____

Religion(s): _____

Language(s): _____

Currency: _____

Climate: _____

Time Zone: _____

Major Exports

1:_____

2:_____

3:_____

Mountains, Rivers and Lakes

1:_____

2:_____

3:_____

Other Cool Things about this Country

1:_____

2:_____

3:_____

4:_____

Bangladesh

Color the country's flag in the box above.

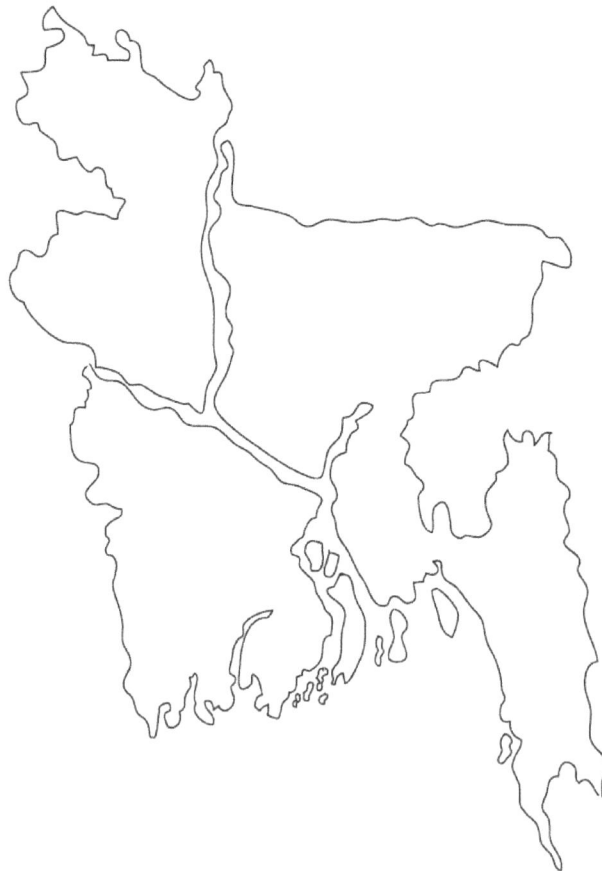

Label the capital city and any major physical features such as mountains, rivers, oceans or seas **in or around** this country.

Country Name: Bangladesh

FACTS

Population:_____

Area: _____

Type of Government: _____

Capital City: _____

Religion(s): _____

Language(s): _____

Currency: _____

Climate: _____

Time Zone: _____

Major Exports

1:_____

2: _____

3: _____

Mountains, Rivers and Lakes

1:_____

2: _____

3: _____

Other Cool Things about this Country

1:_____

2: _____

3: _____

4: _____

Bhutan

Color the country's flag in the box above.

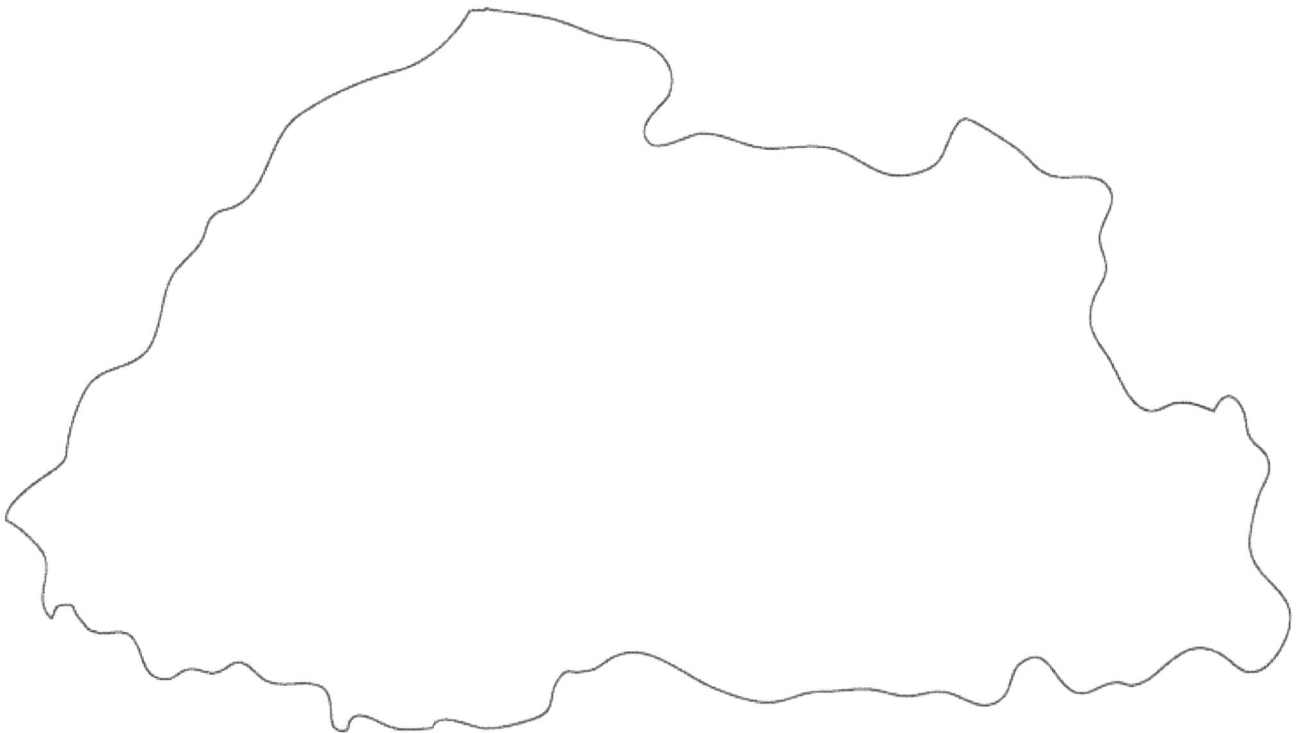

Label the capital city and any major physical features such as mountains, rivers, oceans or seas **in or around** this country.

Country Name: Bhutan

FACTS

Population:_____

Area: _____

Type of Government: _____

Capital City: _____

Religion(s): _____

Language(s): _____

Currency: _____

Climate: _____

Time Zone: _____

Major Exports

1:_____

2:_____

3:_____

Mountains, Rivers and Lakes

1:_____

2:_____

3:_____

Other Cool Things about this Country

1:_____

2:_____

3:_____

4:_____

Brunei

Color the country's flag in the box above.

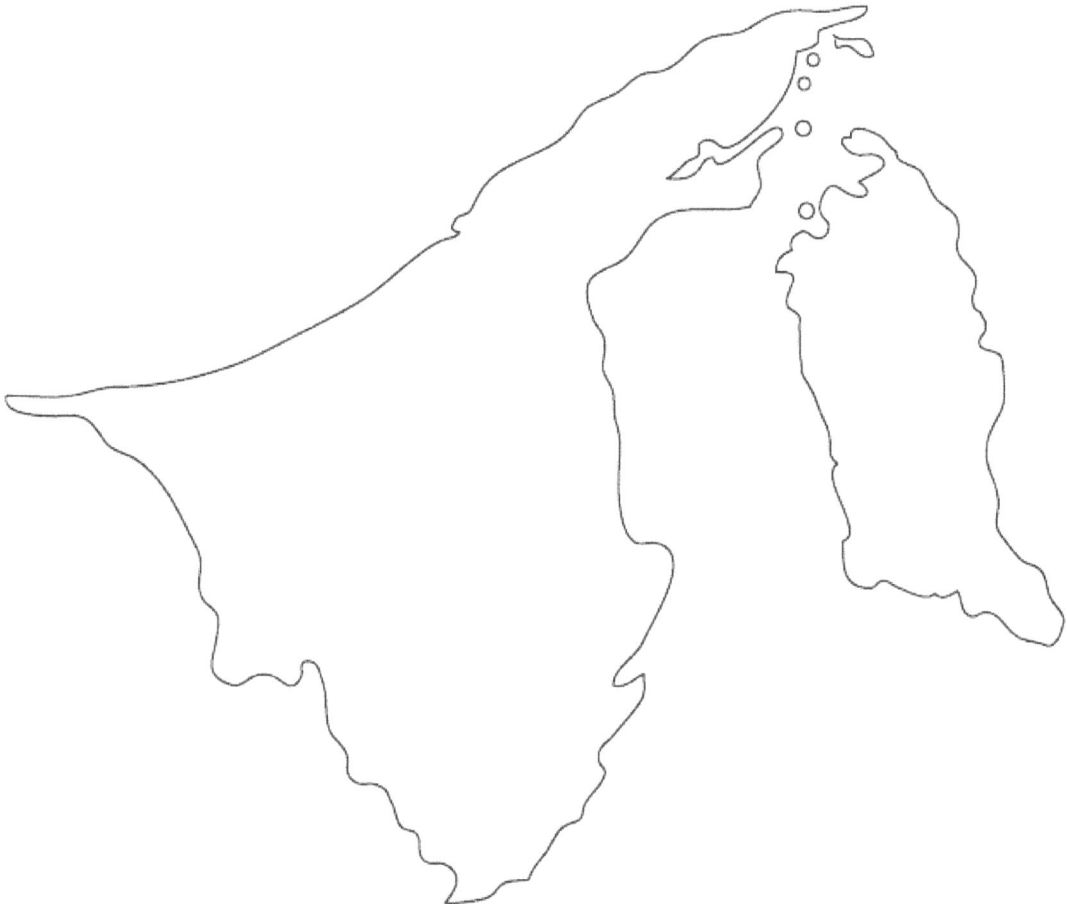

Label the capital city and any major physical features such as mountains, rivers, oceans or seas **in or around** this country.

Country Name: Brunei

FACTS

Population:_____

Area: _____

Type of Government: _____

Capital City: _____

Religion(s): _____

Language(s): _____

Currency: _____

Climate: _____

Time Zone: _____

Major Exports

1:_____

2:_____

3:_____

Mountains, Rivers and Lakes

1:_____

2:_____

3:_____

Other Cool Things about this Country

1:_____

2:_____

3:_____

4:_____

Cambodia

Color the country's flag in the box above.

Label the capital city and any major physical features such as mountains, rivers, oceans or seas **in or around** this country.

Country Name: Cambodia

FACTS

Population:_____

Area: _____

Type of Government: _____

Capital City: _____

Religion(s): _____

Language(s): _____

Currency: _____

Climate: _____

Time Zone: _____

Major Exports

1:_____

2: _____

3: _____

Mountains, Rivers and Lakes

1:_____

2: _____

3: _____

Other Cool Things about this Country

1:_____

2: _____

3: _____

4: _____

China

Color the country's flag in the box above.

Label the capital city and any major physical features such as mountains, rivers, oceans or seas **in or around** this country.

Country Name: China

FACTS

Population:_____

Area: _____

Type of Government: _____

Capital City: _____

Religion(s): _____

Language(s): _____

Currency: _____

Climate: _____

Time Zone: _____

Major Exports

1:_____

2:_____

3:_____

Mountains, Rivers and Lakes

1:_____

2:_____

3:_____

Other Cool Things about this Country

1:_____

2:_____

3:_____

4:_____

Cyprus

Color the country's flag in the box above.

Label the capital city and any major physical features such as mountains, rivers, oceans or seas **in or around** this country.

Country Name: Cyprus

FACTS

Population:_____

Area: _____

Type of Government: _____

Capital City: _____

Religion(s): _____

Language(s): _____

Currency: _____

Climate: _____

Time Zone: _____

Major Exports

1:_____

2: _____

3: _____

Mountains, Rivers and Lakes

1:_____

2: _____

3: _____

Other Cool Things about this Country

1:_____

2: _____

3: _____

4: _____

Georgia

Color the country's flag in the box above.

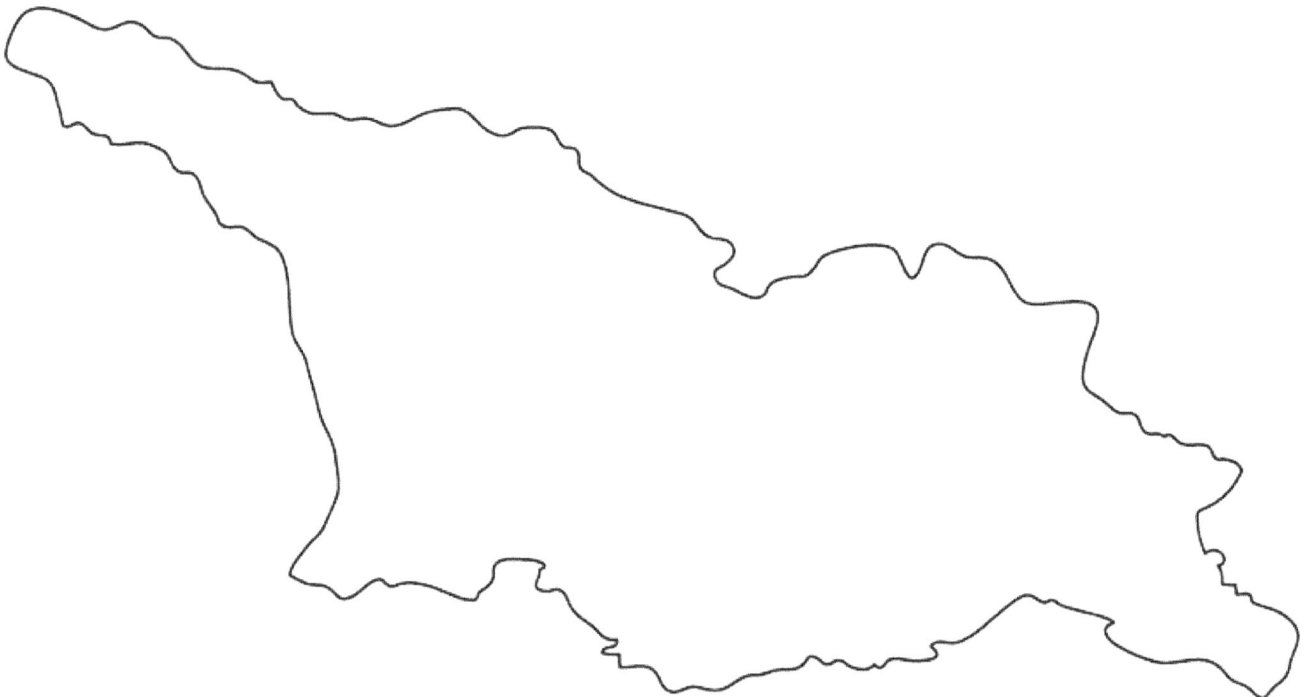

Label the capital city and any major physical features such as mountains, rivers, oceans or seas **in or around** this country.

Country Name: Georgia

FACTS

Population:_____

Area: _____

Type of Government: _____

Capital City: _____

Religion(s): _____

Language(s): _____

Currency: _____

Climate: _____

Time Zone: _____

Major Exports

1:_____

2: _____

3: _____

Mountains, Rivers and Lakes

1:_____

2: _____

3: _____

Other Cool Things about this Country

1:_____

2: _____

3: _____

4: _____

India

Color the country's flag in the box above.

Label the capital city and any major physical features such as mountains, rivers, oceans or seas **in or around** this country.

Country Name: India

FACTS

Population:_____

Area: _____

Type of Government: _____

Capital City: _____

Religion(s): _____

Language(s): _____

Currency: _____

Climate: _____

Time Zone: _____

Major Exports

1:_____

2: _____

3: _____

Mountains, Rivers and Lakes

1:_____

2: _____

3: _____

Other Cool Things about this Country

1:_____

2: _____

3: _____

4: _____

Indonesia

Color the country's flag in the box above.

Label the capital city and any major physical features such as mountains, rivers, oceans or seas **in or around** this country.

Country Name: Indonesia

FACTS

Population:_____

Area: _____

Type of Government: _____

Capital City: _____

Religion(s): _____

Language(s): _____

Currency: _____

Climate: _____

Time Zone: _____

Major Exports

1:_____

2: _____

3: _____

Mountains, Rivers and Lakes

1:_____

2: _____

3: _____

Other Cool Things about this Country

1:_____

2: _____

3: _____

4: _____

Iran

Color the country's flag in the box above.

Label the capital city and any major physical features such as mountains, rivers, oceans or seas **in or around** this country.

Country Name: Iran

FACTS

Population:_____

Area: _____

Type of Government: _____

Capital City: _____

Religion(s): _____

Language(s): _____

Currency: _____

Climate: _____

Time Zone: _____

Major Exports

1:_____

2: _____

3: _____

Mountains, Rivers and Lakes

1:_____

2: _____

3: _____

Other Cool Things about this Country

1:_____

2: _____

3: _____

4: _____

Iraq

Color the country's flag in the box above.

Label the capital city and any major physical features such as mountains, rivers, oceans or seas **in or around** this country.

Country Name: Iraq

FACTS

Population:_____

Area: _____

Type of Government: _____

Capital City: _____

Religion(s): _____

Language(s): _____

Currency: _____

Climate: _____

Time Zone: _____

Major Exports

1:_____

2: _____

3: _____

Mountains, Rivers and Lakes

1:_____

2: _____

3: _____

Other Cool Things about this Country

1:_____

2: _____

3: _____

4: _____

Israel

Color the country's flag in the box above.

Label the capital city and any major physical features such as mountains, rivers, oceans or seas **in or around** this country.

Country Name: Israel

FACTS

Population:_____

Area: _____

Type of Government: _____

Capital City: _____

Religion(s): _____

Language(s): _____

Currency: _____

Climate: _____

Time Zone: _____

Major Exports

1:_____

2: _____

3: _____

Mountains, Rivers and Lakes

1:_____

2: _____

3: _____

Other Cool Things about this Country

1:_____

2: _____

3: _____

4: _____

Japan

Color the country's flag in the box above.

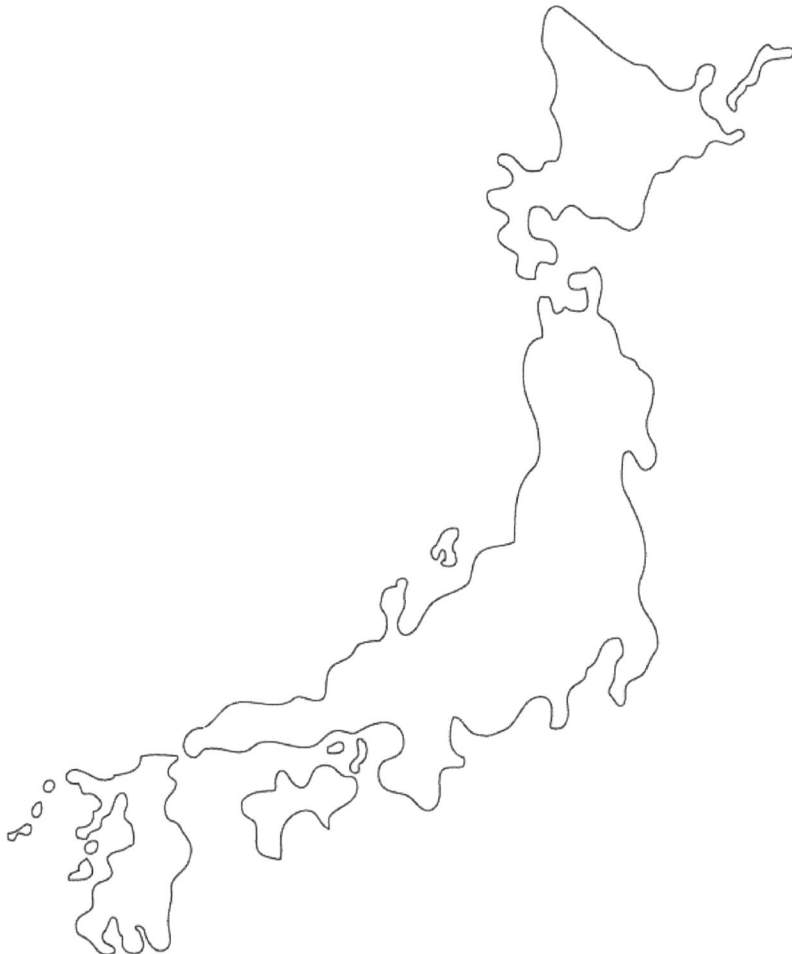

Label the capital city and any major physical features such as mountains, rivers, oceans or seas **in or around** this country.

Country Name: Japan

FACTS

Population:_____

Area: _____

Type of Government: _____

Capital City: _____

Religion(s): _____

Language(s): _____

Currency: _____

Climate: _____

Time Zone: _____

Major Exports

1:_____

2: _____

3: _____

Mountains, Rivers and Lakes

1:_____

2: _____

3: _____

Other Cool Things about this Country

1:_____

2: _____

3: _____

4: _____

Jordan

Color the country's flag in the box above.

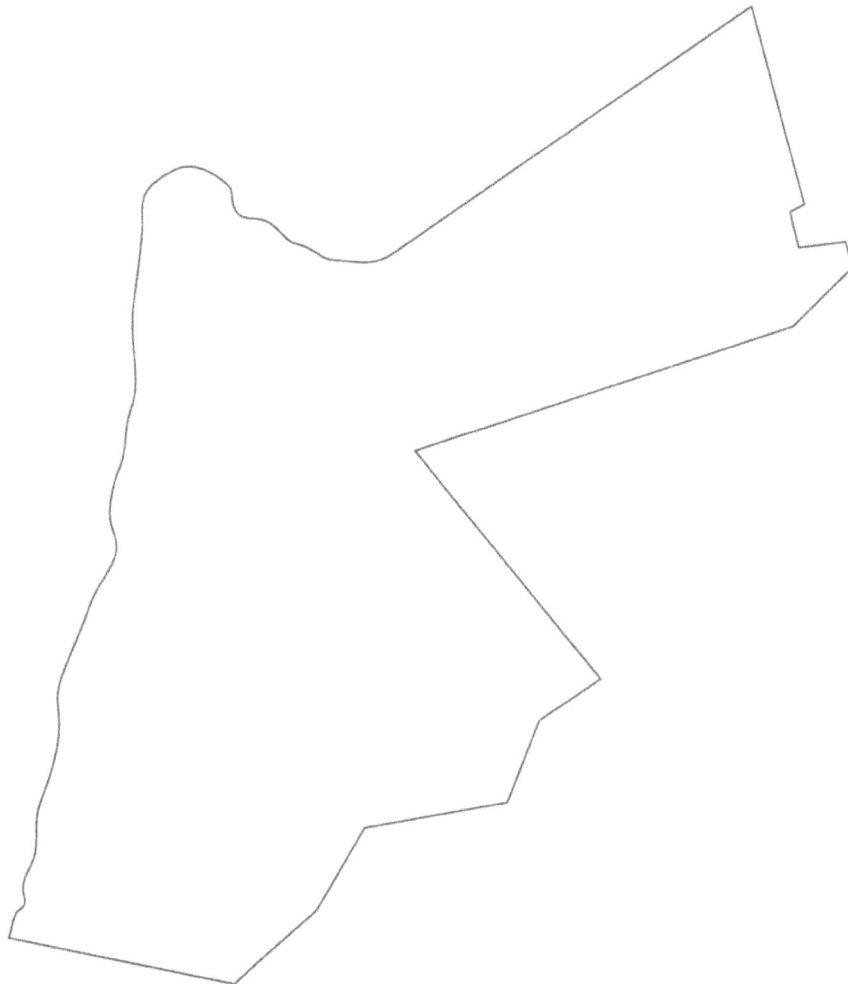

Label the capital city and any major physical features such as mountains, rivers, oceans or seas **in or around** this country.

Country Name: Jordan

FACTS

Population:_____

Area: _____

Type of Government: _____

Capital City: _____

Religion(s): _____

Language(s): _____

Currency: _____

Climate: _____

Time Zone: _____

Major Exports

1:_____

2: _____

3: _____

Mountains, Rivers and Lakes

1:_____

2: _____

3: _____

Other Cool Things about this Country

1:_____

2: _____

3: _____

4: _____

Kazakhstan

Color the country's flag in the box above.

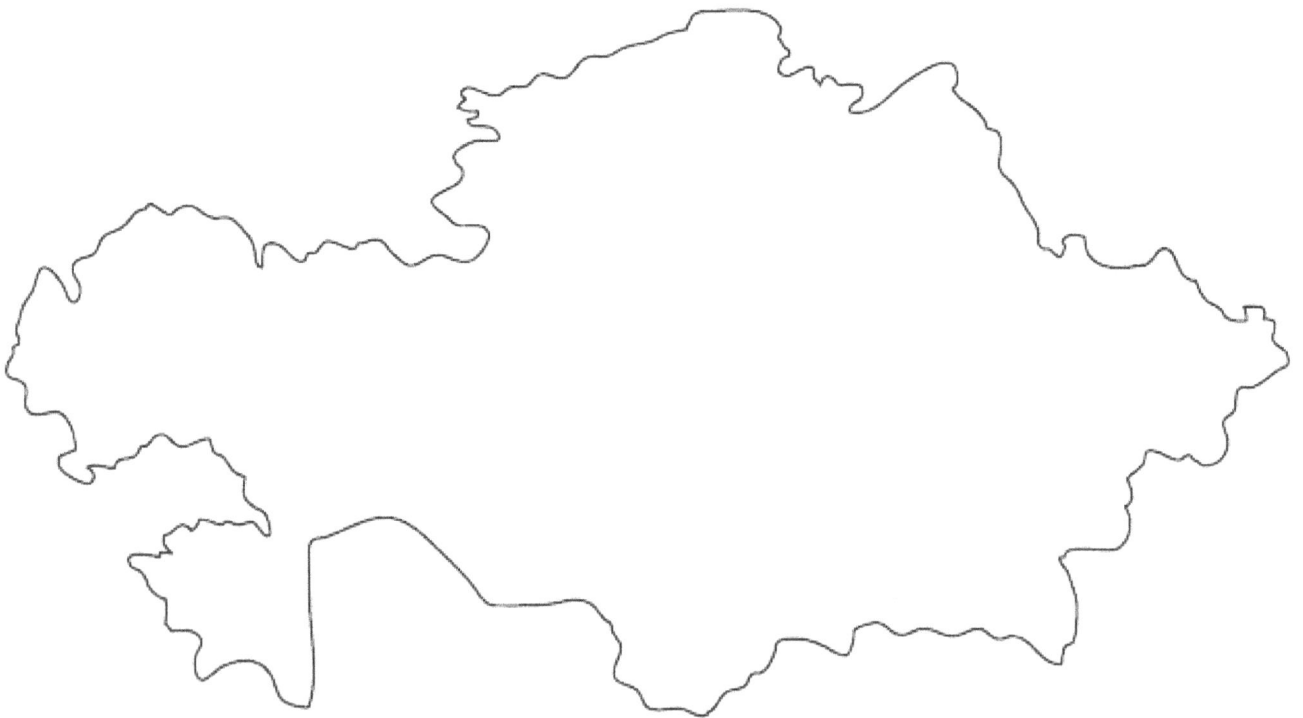

Label the capital city and any major physical features such as mountains, rivers, oceans or seas **in or around** this country.

Country Name: Kazakhstan

FACTS

Population:_____

Area: _____

Type of Government: _____

Capital City: _____

Religion(s): _____

Language(s): _____

Currency: _____

Climate: _____

Time Zone: _____

Major Exports

1:_____

2:_____

3:_____

Mountains, Rivers and Lakes

1:_____

2:_____

3:_____

Other Cool Things about this Country

1:_____

2:_____

3:_____

4:_____

Kuwait

Color the country's flag in the box above.

Label the capital city and any major physical features such as mountains, rivers, oceans or seas **in or around** this country.

Country Name: Kuwait

FACTS

Population:_____

Area: _____

Type of Government: _____

Capital City: _____

Religion(s): _____

Language(s): _____

Currency: _____

Climate: _____

Time Zone: _____

Major Exports

1:_____

2: _____

3: _____

Mountains, Rivers and Lakes

1:_____

2: _____

3: _____

Other Cool Things about this Country

1:_____

2: _____

3: _____

4: _____

Kyrgyzstan

Color the country's flag in the box above.

Label the capital city and any major physical features such as mountains, rivers, oceans or seas **in or around** this country.

Country Name: Kyrgyzstan

FACTS

Population:_____

Area: _____

Type of Government: _____

Capital City: _____

Religion(s): _____

Language(s): _____

Currency: _____

Climate: _____

Time Zone: _____

Major Exports

1:_____

2:_____

3:_____

Mountains, Rivers and Lakes

1:_____

2:_____

3:_____

Other Cool Things about this Country

1:_____

2:_____

3:_____

4:_____

Laos

Color the country's flag in the box above.

Label the capital city and any major physical features such as mountains, rivers, oceans or seas **in or around** this country.

Country Name: Laos

FACTS

Population:_____

Area: _____

Type of Government: _____

Capital City: _____

Religion(s): _____

Language(s): _____

Currency: _____

Climate: _____

Time Zone: _____

Major Exports

1:_____

2: _____

3: _____

Mountains, Rivers and Lakes

1:_____

2: _____

3: _____

Other Cool Things about this Country

1:_____

2: _____

3: _____

4: _____

Lebanon

Color the country's flag in the box above.

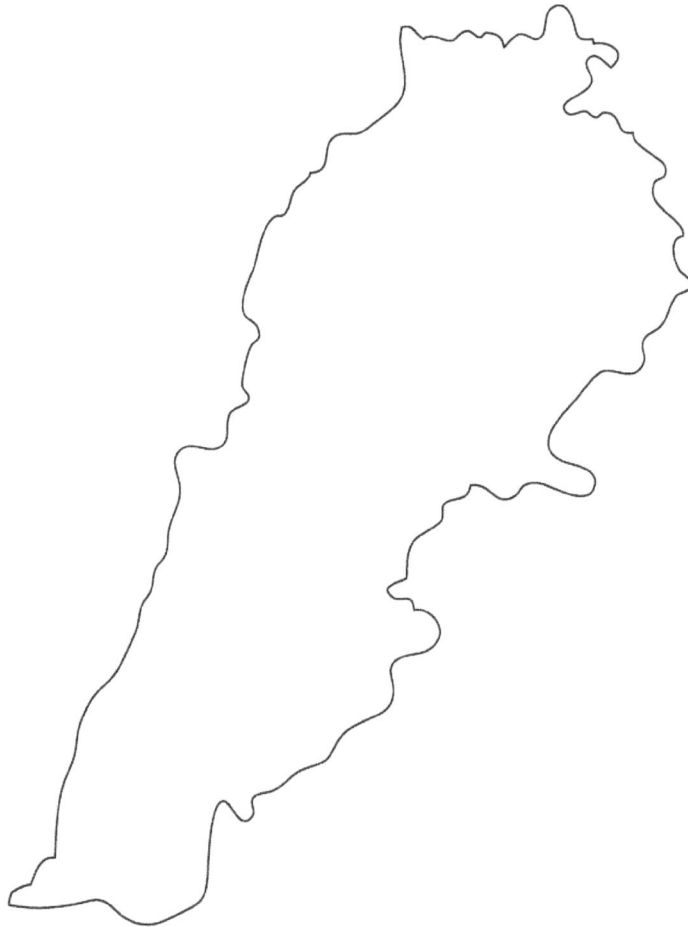

Label the capital city and any major physical features such as mountains, rivers, oceans or seas **in or around** this country.

Country Name: Lebanon

FACTS

Population:_____

Area: _____

Type of Government: _____

Capital City: _____

Religion(s): _____

Language(s): _____

Currency: _____

Climate: _____

Time Zone: _____

Major Exports

1:_____

2: _____

3: _____

Mountains, Rivers and Lakes

1:_____

2: _____

3: _____

Other Cool Things about this Country

1:_____

2: _____

3: _____

4: _____

Malaysia

Color the country's flag in the box above.

Label the capital city and any major physical features such as mountains, rivers, oceans or seas **in or around** this country.

Country Name: Malaysia

FACTS

Population:_____

Area: _____

Type of Government: _____

Capital City: _____

Religion(s): _____

Language(s): _____

Currency: _____

Climate: _____

Time Zone: _____

Major Exports

1:_____

2:_____

3:_____

Mountains, Rivers and Lakes

1:_____

2:_____

3:_____

Other Cool Things about this Country

1:_____

2:_____

3:_____

4:_____

Maldives

Color the country's flag in the box above.

Label the capital city and any major physical features such as mountains, rivers, oceans or seas **in or around** this country.

Country Name: Maldives

FACTS

Population:_____

Area: _____

Type of Government: _____

Capital City: _____

Religion(s): _____

Language(s): _____

Currency: _____

Climate: _____

Time Zone: _____

Major Exports

1:_____

2: _____

3: _____

Mountains, Rivers and Lakes

1:_____

2: _____

3: _____

Other Cool Things about this Country

1:_____

2: _____

3: _____

4: _____

Mongolia

Color the country's flag in the box above.

Label the capital city and any major physical features such as mountains, rivers, oceans or seas **in or around** this country.

Country Name: Mongolia

FACTS

Population:_____

Area: _____

Type of Government: _____

Capital City: _____

Religion(s): _____

Language(s): _____

Currency: _____

Climate: _____

Time Zone: _____

Major Exports

1:_____

2:_____

3:_____

Mountains, Rivers and Lakes

1:_____

2:_____

3:_____

Other Cool Things about this Country

1:_____

2:_____

3:_____

4:_____

Myanmar

Color the country's flag in the box above.

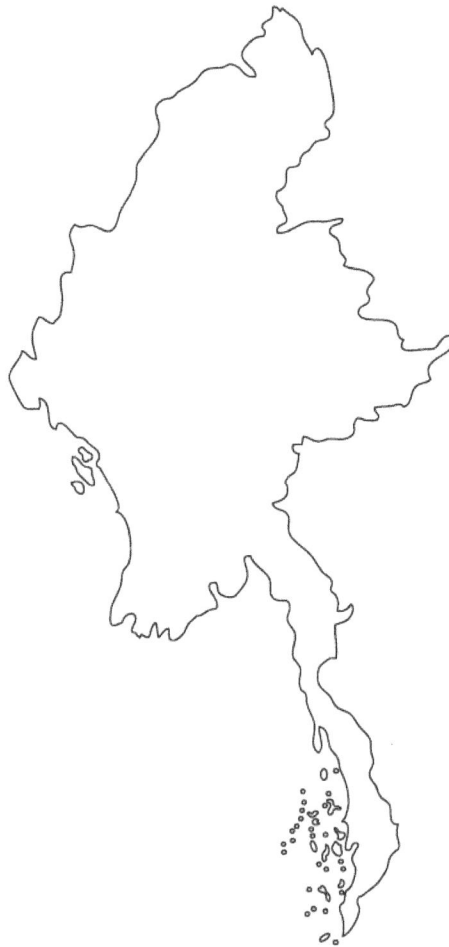

Label the capital city and any major physical features such as mountains, rivers, oceans or seas **in or around** this country.

Country Name: Myanmar

FACTS

Population:_____

Area: _____

Type of Government: _____

Capital City: _____

Religion(s): _____

Language(s): _____

Currency: _____

Climate: _____

Time Zone: _____

Major Exports

1:_____

2: _____

3: _____

Mountains, Rivers and Lakes

1:_____

2: _____

3: _____

Other Cool Things about this Country

1:_____

2:_____

3:_____

4:_____

Nepal

Color the country's flag in the box above.

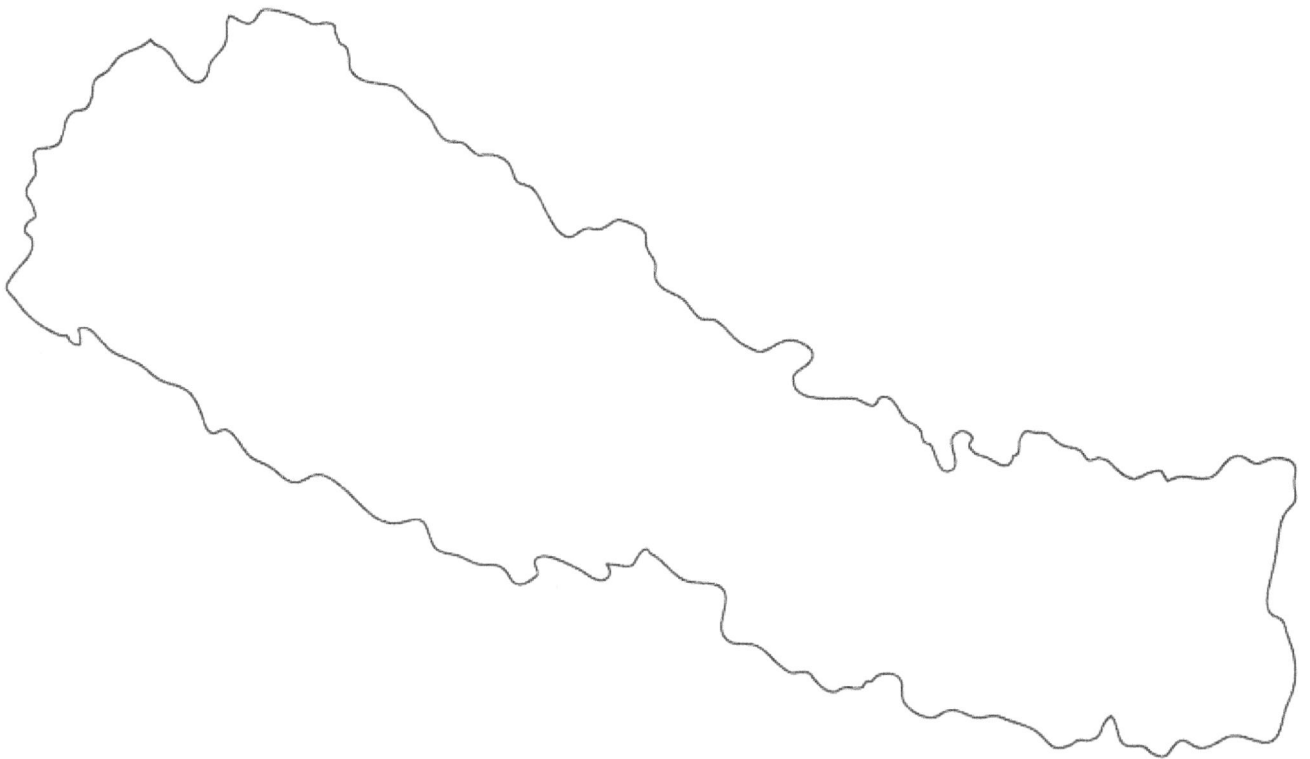

Label the capital city and any major physical features such as mountains, rivers, oceans or seas **in or around** this country.

Country Name: Nepal

FACTS

Population:_____

Area: _____

Type of Government: _____

Capital City: _____

Religion(s): _____

Language(s): _____

Currency: _____

Climate: _____

Time Zone: _____

Major Exports

1:_____

2: _____

3: _____

Mountains, Rivers and Lakes

1:_____

2: _____

3: _____

Other Cool Things about this Country

1:_____

2: _____

3: _____

4: _____

North Korea

Color the country's flag in the box above.

Label the capital city and any major physical features such as mountains, rivers, oceans or seas **in or around** this country.

Country Name: North Korea

FACTS

Population:_____

Area: _____

Type of Government: _____

Capital City: _____

Religion(s): _____

Language(s): _____

Currency: _____

Climate: _____

Time Zone: _____

Major Exports

1:_____

2:_____

3:_____

Mountains, Rivers and Lakes

1:_____

2:_____

3:_____

Other Cool Things about this Country

1:_____

2:_____

3:_____

4:_____

Oman

Color the country's flag in the box above.

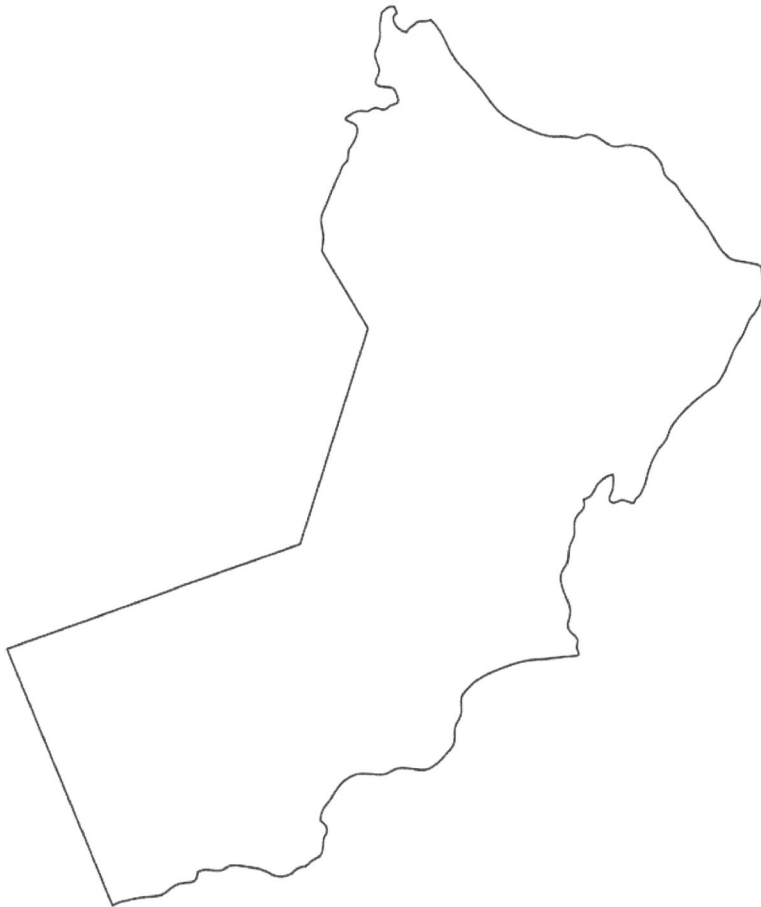

Label the capital city and any major physical features such as mountains, rivers, oceans or seas **in or around** this country.

Country Name: Oman

FACTS

Population:_____

Area: _____

Type of Government: _____

Capital City: _____

Religion(s): _____

Language(s): _____

Currency: _____

Climate: _____

Time Zone: _____

Major Exports

1:_____

2: _____

3: _____

Mountains, Rivers and Lakes

1:_____

2: _____

3: _____

Other Cool Things about this Country

1:_____

2: _____

3: _____

4: _____

Pakistan

Color the country's flag in the box above.

Label the capital city and any major physical features such as mountains, rivers, oceans or seas **in or around** this country.

Country Name: Pakistan

FACTS

Population:_____

Area: _____

Type of Government: _____

Capital City: _____

Religion(s): _____

Language(s): _____

Currency: _____

Climate: _____

Time Zone: _____

Major Exports

1:_____

2: _____

3: _____

Mountains, Rivers and Lakes

1:_____

2: _____

3: _____

Other Cool Things about this Country

1:_____

2: _____

3: _____

4: _____

Palestine State

Color the country's flag in the box above.

Label the capital city and any major physical features such as mountains, rivers, oceans or seas **in or around** this country.

Country Name: Palestine State

FACTS

Population:_____

Area: _____

Type of Government: _____

Capital City: _____

Religion(s): _____

Language(s): _____

Currency: _____

Climate: _____

Time Zone: _____

Major Exports

1:_____

2: _____

3: _____

Mountains, Rivers and Lakes

1:_____

2: _____

3: _____

Other Cool Things about this Country

1:_____

2: _____

3: _____

4: _____

Philippines

Color the country's flag in the box above.

Label the capital city and any major physical features such as mountains, rivers, oceans or seas **in or around** this country.

Country Name: Philippines

FACTS

Population:_____

Area: _____

Type of Government: _____

Capital City: _____

Religion(s): _____

Language(s): _____

Currency: _____

Climate: _____

Time Zone: _____

Major Exports

1:_____

2: _____

3: _____

Mountains, Rivers and Lakes

1:_____

2: _____

3: _____

Other Cool Things about this Country

1:_____

2: _____

3: _____

4: _____

Qatar

Color the country's flag in the box above.

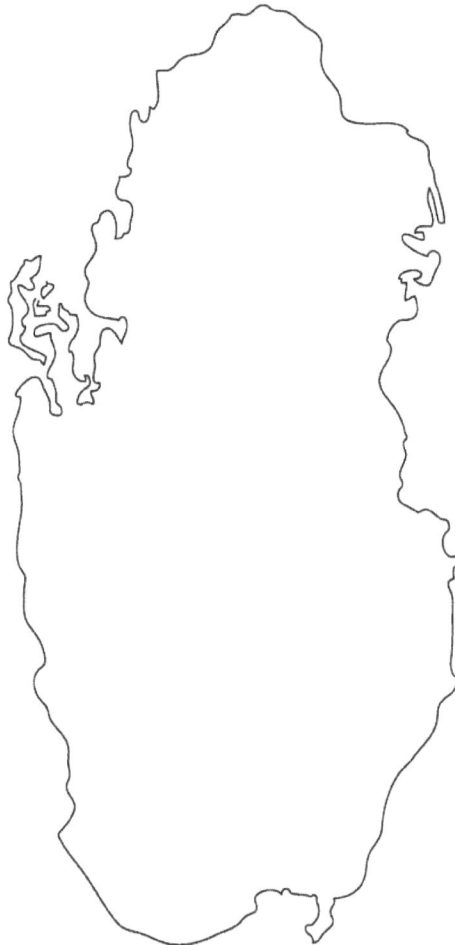

Label the capital city and any major physical features such as mountains, rivers, oceans or seas **in or around** this country.

Country Name: Qatar

FACTS

Population:_____

Area: _____

Type of Government: _____

Capital City: _____

Religion(s): _____

Language(s): _____

Currency: _____

Climate: _____

Time Zone: _____

Major Exports

1:_____

2: _____

3: _____

Mountains, Rivers and Lakes

1:_____

2: _____

3: _____

Other Cool Things about this Country

1:_____

2: _____

3: _____

4: _____

Russia

Color the country's flag in the box above.

Label the capital city and any major physical features such as mountains, rivers, oceans or seas **in or around** this country.

Country Name: Russia

FACTS

Population:_____

Area: _____

Type of Government: _____

Capital City: _____

Religion(s): _____

Language(s): _____

Currency: _____

Climate: _____

Time Zone: _____

Major Exports

1:_____

2: _____

3: _____

Mountains, Rivers and Lakes

1:_____

2: _____

3: _____

Other Cool Things about this Country

1:_____

2: _____

3: _____

4: _____

Saudi Arabia

Color the country's flag in the box above.

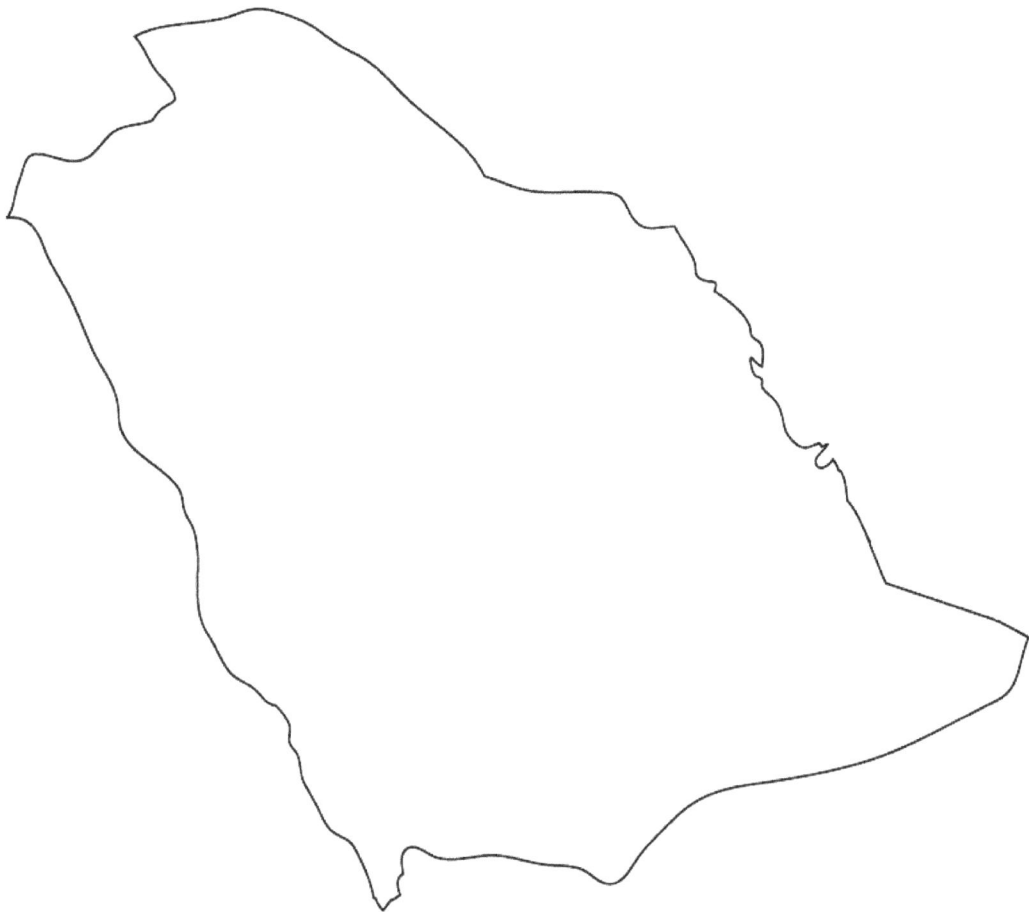

Label the capital city and any major physical features such as mountains, rivers, oceans or seas **in or around** this country.

Country Name: Saudi Arabia

FACTS

Population:_____

Area: _____

Type of Government: _____

Capital City: _____

Religion(s): _____

Language(s): _____

Currency: _____

Climate: _____

Time Zone: _____

Major Exports

1:_____

2: _____

3: _____

Mountains, Rivers and Lakes

1:_____

2: _____

3: _____

Other Cool Things about this Country

1:_____

2: _____

3: _____

4: _____

Singapore

Color the country's flag in the box above.

Label the capital city and any major physical features such as mountains, rivers, oceans or seas **in or around** this country.

Country Name: Singapore

FACTS

Population:_____

Area: _____

Type of Government: _____

Capital City: _____

Religion(s): _____

Language(s): _____

Currency: _____

Climate: _____

Time Zone: _____

Major Exports

1:_____

2: _____

3: _____

Mountains, Rivers and Lakes

1:_____

2: _____

3: _____

Other Cool Things about this Country

1:_____

2: _____

3: _____

4: _____

South Korea

Color the country's flag in the box above.

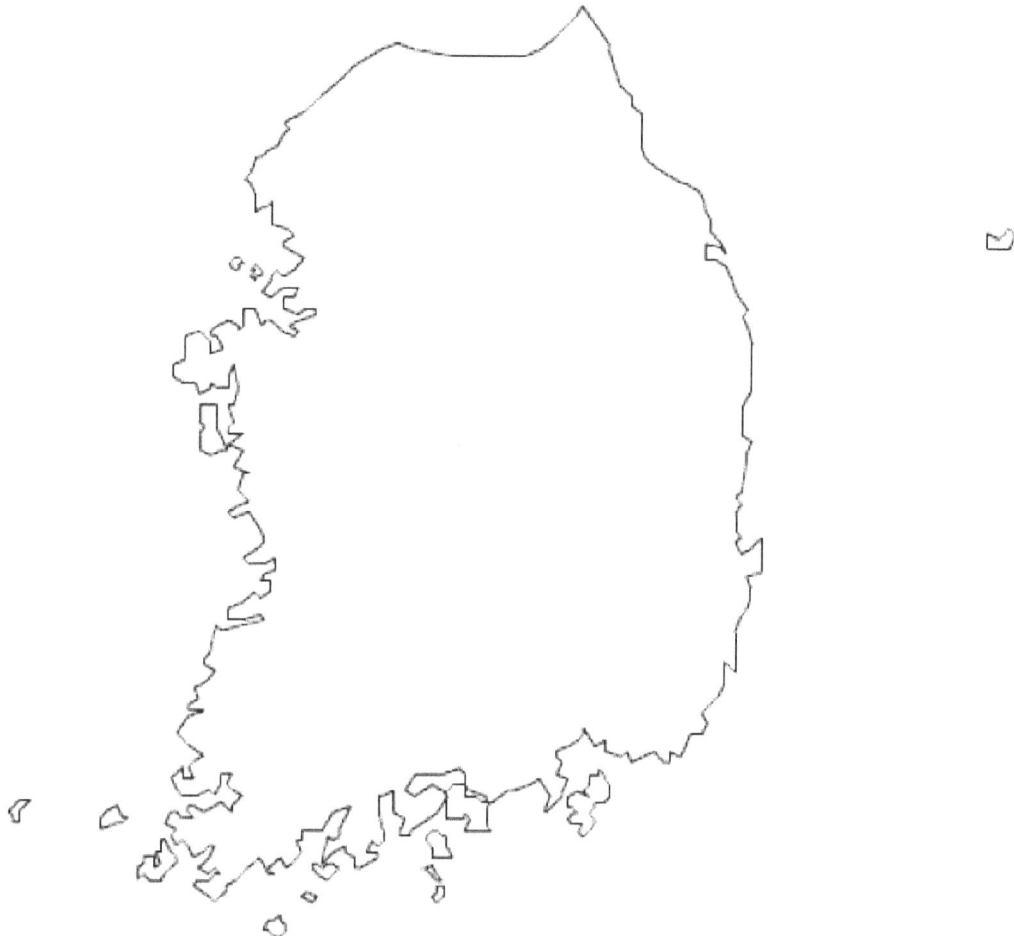

Label the capital city and any major physical features such as mountains, rivers, oceans or seas **in or around** this country.

Country Name: South Korea

FACTS

Population:_____

Area: _____

Type of Government: _____

Capital City: _____

Religion(s): _____

Language(s): _____

Currency: _____

Climate: _____

Time Zone: _____

Major Exports

1:_____

2: _____

3: _____

Mountains, Rivers and Lakes

1:_____

2: _____

3: _____

Other Cool Things about this Country

1:_____

2: _____

3: _____

4: _____

Sri Lanka

Color the country's flag in the box above.

Label the capital city and any major physical features such as mountains, rivers, oceans or seas **in or around** this country.

Country Name: Sri Lanka

FACTS

Population:_____

Area: _____

Type of Government: _____

Capital City: _____

Religion(s): _____

Language(s): _____

Currency: _____

Climate: _____

Time Zone: _____

Major Exports

1:_____

2:_____

3:_____

Mountains, Rivers and Lakes

1:_____

2:_____

3:_____

Other Cool Things about this Country

1:_____

2:_____

3:_____

4:_____

Syria

Color the country's flag in the box above.

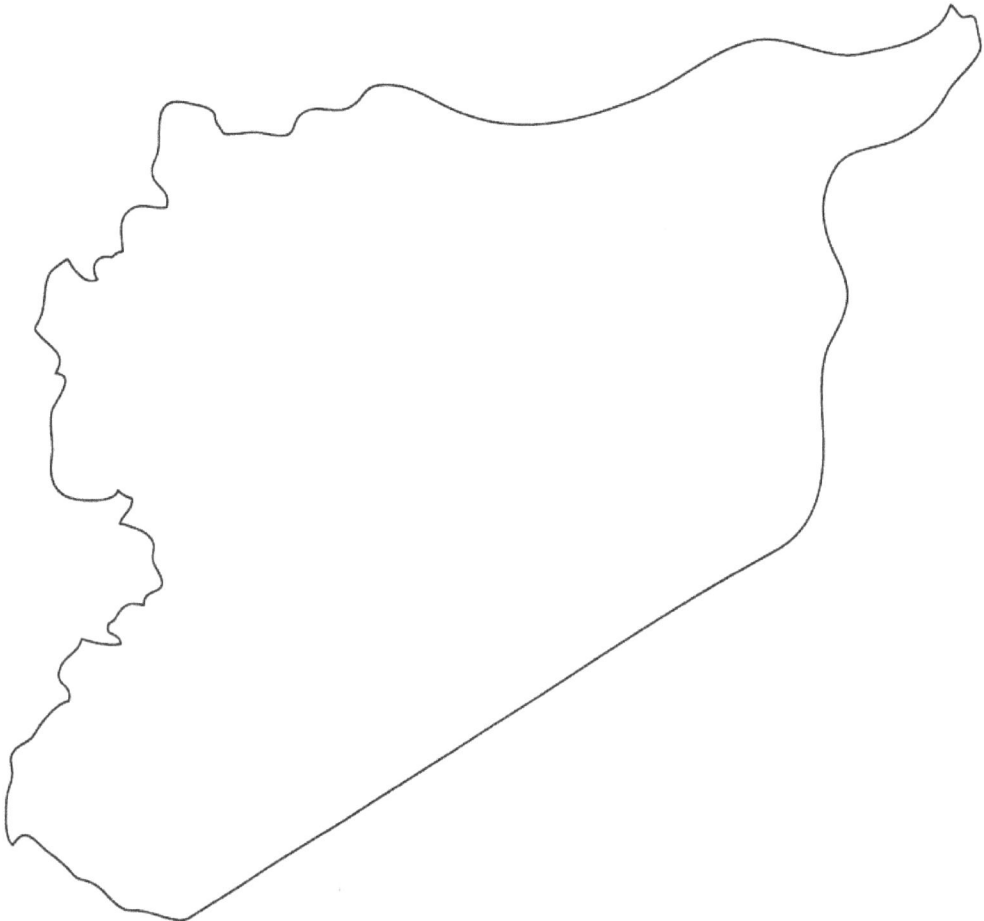

Label the capital city and any major physical features such as mountains, rivers, oceans or seas **in or around** this country.

Country Name: Syria

FACTS

Population:_____

Area: _____

Type of Government: _____

Capital City: _____

Religion(s): _____

Language(s): _____

Currency: _____

Climate: _____

Time Zone: _____

Major Exports

1:_____

2:_____

3:_____

Mountains, Rivers and Lakes

1:_____

2:_____

3:_____

Other Cool Things about this Country

1:_____

2:_____

3:_____

4:_____

Taiwan

Color the country's flag in the box above.

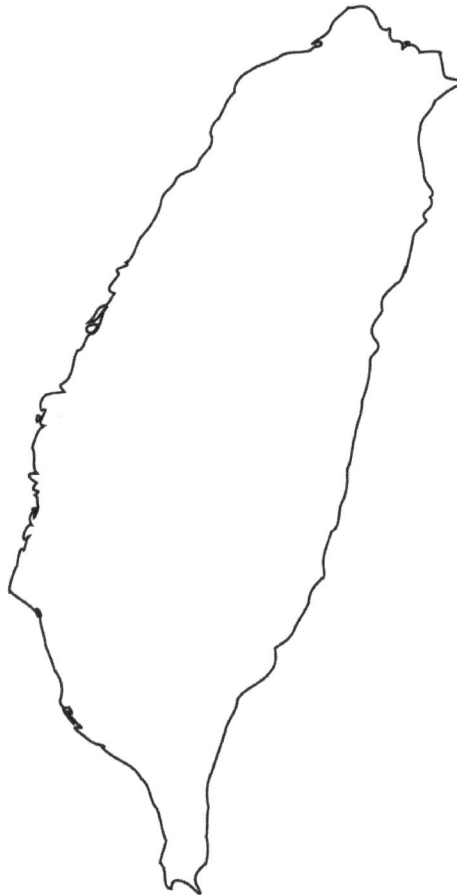

Label the capital city and any major physical features such as mountains, rivers, oceans or seas **in or around** this country.

Country Name: Taiwan

FACTS

Population:_____

Area: _____

Type of Government: _____

Capital City: _____

Religion(s): _____

Language(s): _____

Currency: _____

Climate: _____

Time Zone: _____

Major Exports

1:_____

2: _____

3: _____

Mountains, Rivers and Lakes

1:_____

2: _____

3: _____

Other Cool Things about this Country

1:_____

2: _____

3: _____

4: _____

Tajikistan

Color the country's flag in the box above.

Label the capital city and any major physical features such as mountains, rivers, oceans or seas **in or around** this country.

Country Name: Tajikistan

FACTS

Population:_____

Area: _____

Type of Government: _____

Capital City: _____

Religion(s): _____

Language(s): _____

Currency: _____

Climate: _____

Time Zone: _____

Major Exports

1:_____

2: _____

3: _____

Mountains, Rivers and Lakes

1:_____

2: _____

3: _____

Other Cool Things about this Country

1:_____

2: _____

3: _____

4: _____

Thailand

Color the country's flag in the box above.

Label the capital city and any major physical features such as mountains, rivers, oceans or seas **in or around** this country.

Country Name: Thailand

FACTS

Population:_____

Area: _____

Type of Government: _____

Capital City: _____

Religion(s): _____

Language(s): _____

Currency: _____

Climate: _____

Time Zone: _____

Major Exports

1:_____

2:_____

3:_____

Mountains, Rivers and Lakes

1:_____

2:_____

3:_____

Other Cool Things about this Country

1:_____

2:_____

3:_____

4:_____

Timor-Leste

Color the country's flag in the box above.

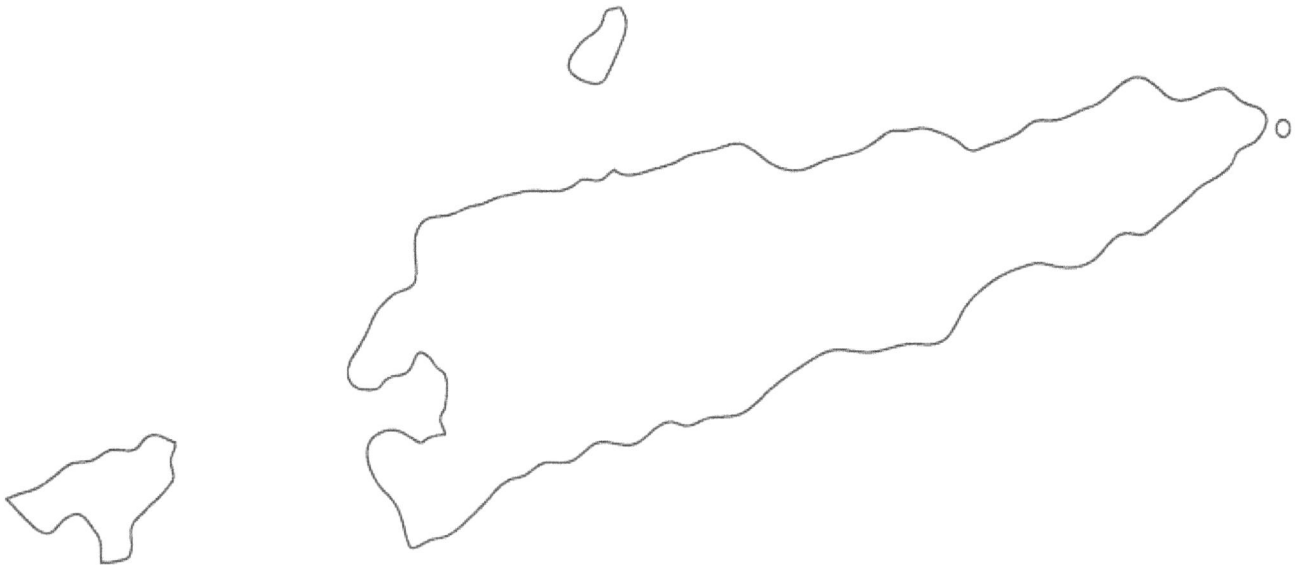

Label the capital city and any major physical features such as mountains, rivers, oceans or seas **in or around** this country.

Country Name: Timor-Leste

FACTS

Population:_____

Area: _____

Type of Government: _____

Capital City: _____

Religion(s): _____

Language(s): _____

Currency: _____

Climate: _____

Time Zone: _____

Major Exports

1:_____

2: _____

3: _____

Mountains, Rivers and Lakes

1:_____

2: _____

3: _____

Other Cool Things about this Country

1:_____

2: _____

3: _____

4: _____

Turkey

Color the country's flag in the box above.

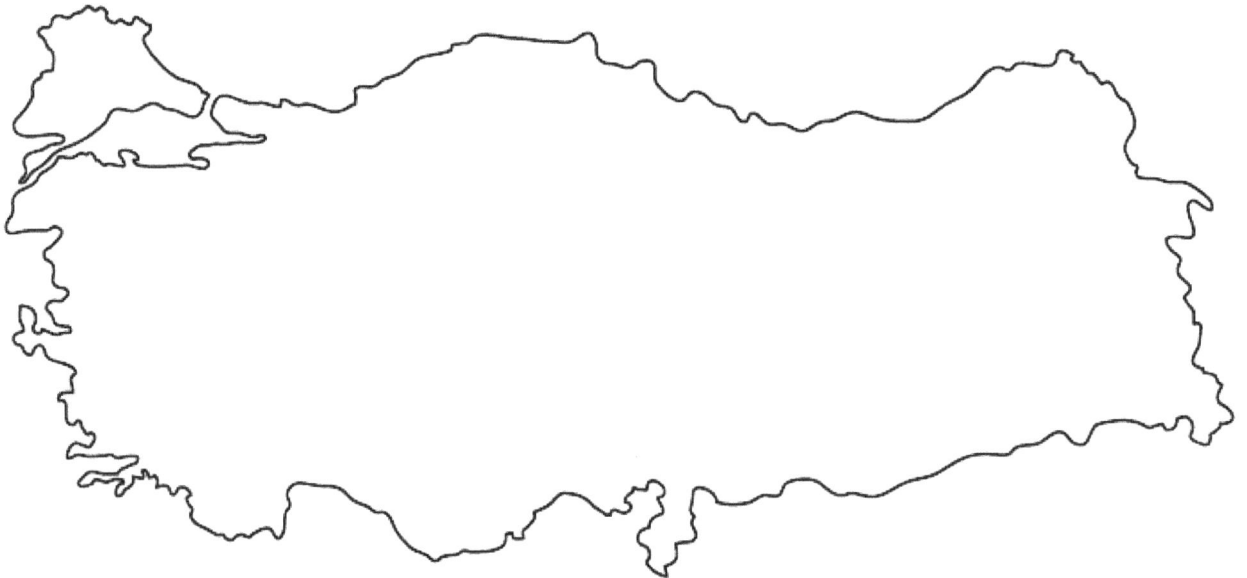

Label the capital city and any major physical features such as mountains, rivers, oceans or seas **in or around** this country.

Country Name: Turkey

FACTS

Population:_____

Area: _____

Type of Government: _____

Capital City: _____

Religion(s): _____

Language(s): _____

Currency: _____

Climate: _____

Time Zone: _____

Major Exports

1:_____

2: _____

3: _____

Mountains, Rivers and Lakes

1:_____

2: _____

3: _____

Other Cool Things about this Country

1:_____

2: _____

3: _____

4: _____

Turkmenistan

Color the country's flag in the box above.

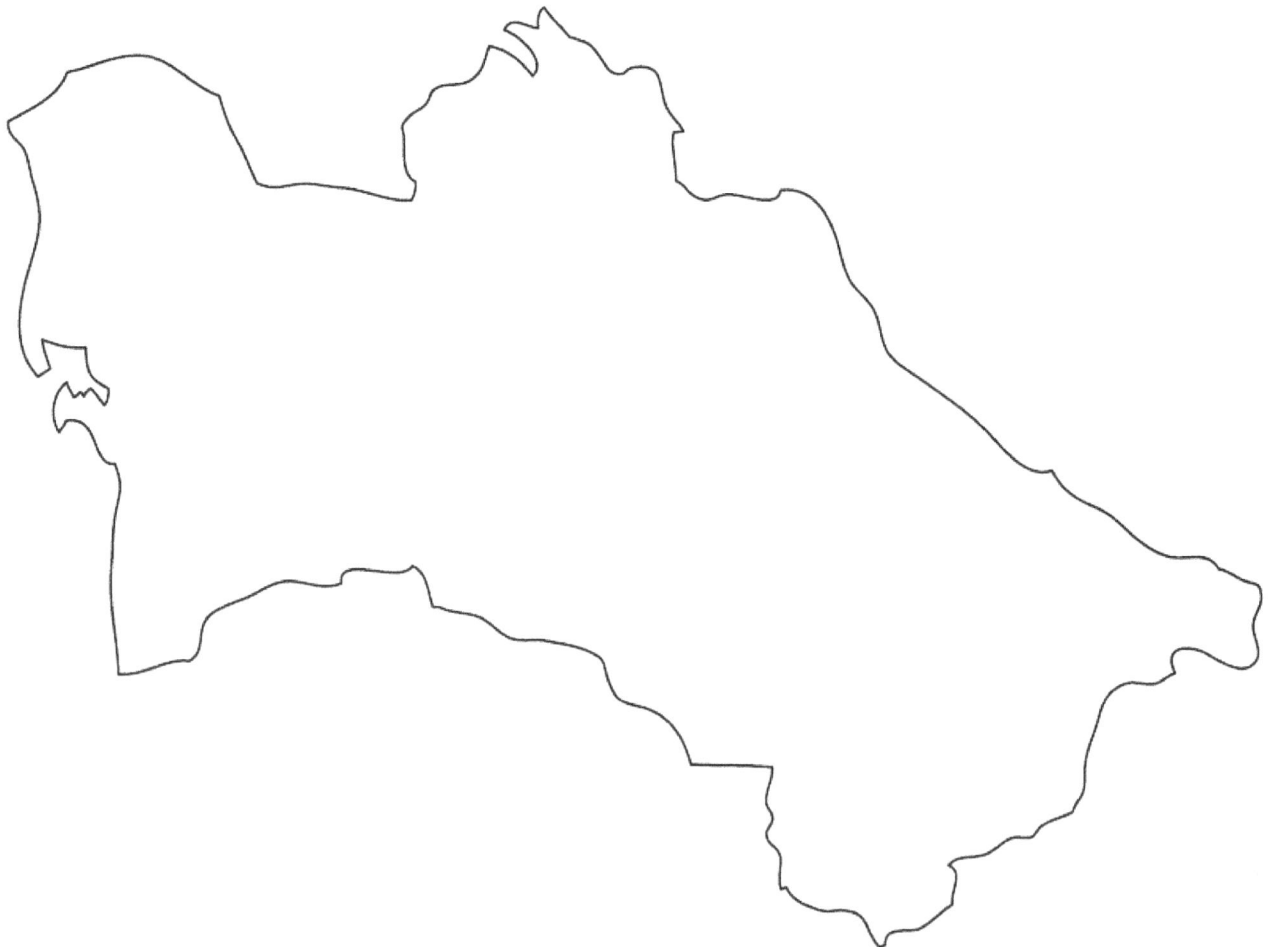

Label the capital city and any major physical features such as mountains, rivers, oceans or seas **in or around** this country.

Country Name: Turkmenistan

FACTS

Population:_____

Area: _____

Type of Government: _____

Capital City: _____

Religion(s): _____

Language(s): _____

Currency: _____

Climate: _____

Time Zone: _____

Major Exports

1:_____

2:_____

3:_____

Mountains, Rivers and Lakes

1:_____

2:_____

3:_____

Other Cool Things about this Country

1:_____

2:_____

3:_____

4:_____

United Arab Emirates

Color the country's flag in the box above.

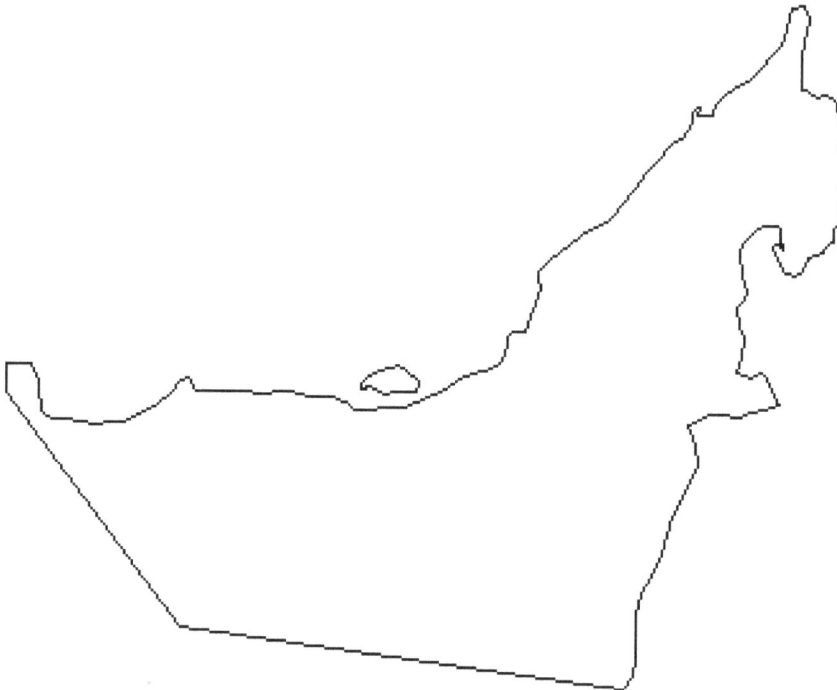

Label the capital city and any major physical features such as mountains, rivers, oceans or seas **in or around** this country.

Country Name: United Arab Emirates

FACTS

Population:_____

Area: _____

Type of Government: _____

Capital City: _____

Religion(s): _____

Language(s): _____

Currency: _____

Climate: _____

Time Zone: _____

Major Exports

1:_____

2: _____

3: _____

Mountains, Rivers and Lakes

1:_____

2: _____

3: _____

Other Cool Things about this Country

1:_____

2: _____

3: _____

4: _____

Uzbekistan

Color the country's flag in the box above.

Label the capital city and any major physical features such as mountains, rivers, oceans or seas **in or around** this country.

Country Name: Uzbekistan

FACTS

Population:_____

Area: _____

Type of Government: _____

Capital City: _____

Religion(s): _____

Language(s): _____

Currency: _____

Climate: _____

Time Zone: _____

Major Exports

1:_____

2: _____

3: _____

Mountains, Rivers and Lakes

1:_____

2: _____

3: _____

Other Cool Things about this Country

1:_____

2: _____

3: _____

4: _____

Vietnam

Color the country's flag in the box above.

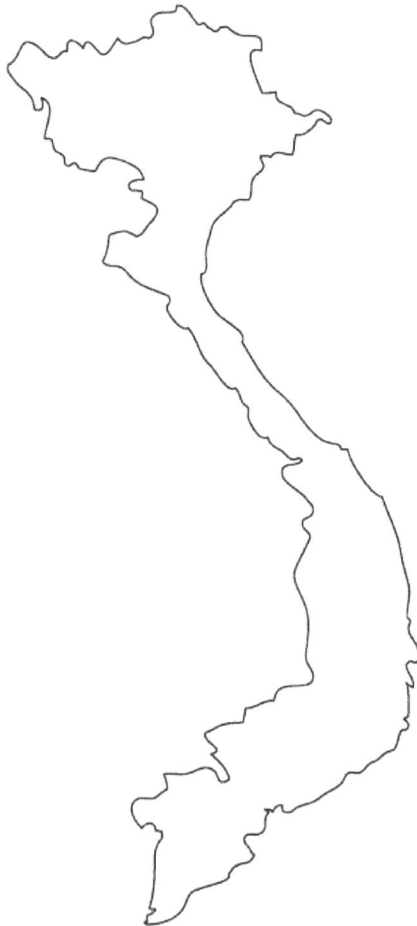

Label the capital city and any major physical features such as mountains, rivers, oceans or seas **in or around** this country.

Country Name: Vietnam

FACTS

Population:_____

Area: _____

Type of Government: _____

Capital City: _____

Religion(s): _____

Language(s): _____

Currency: _____

Climate: _____

Time Zone: _____

Major Exports

1:_____

2:_____

3:_____

Mountains, Rivers and Lakes

1:_____

2:_____

3:_____

Other Cool Things about this Country

1:_____

2:_____

3:_____

4:_____

Yemen

Color the country's flag in the box above.

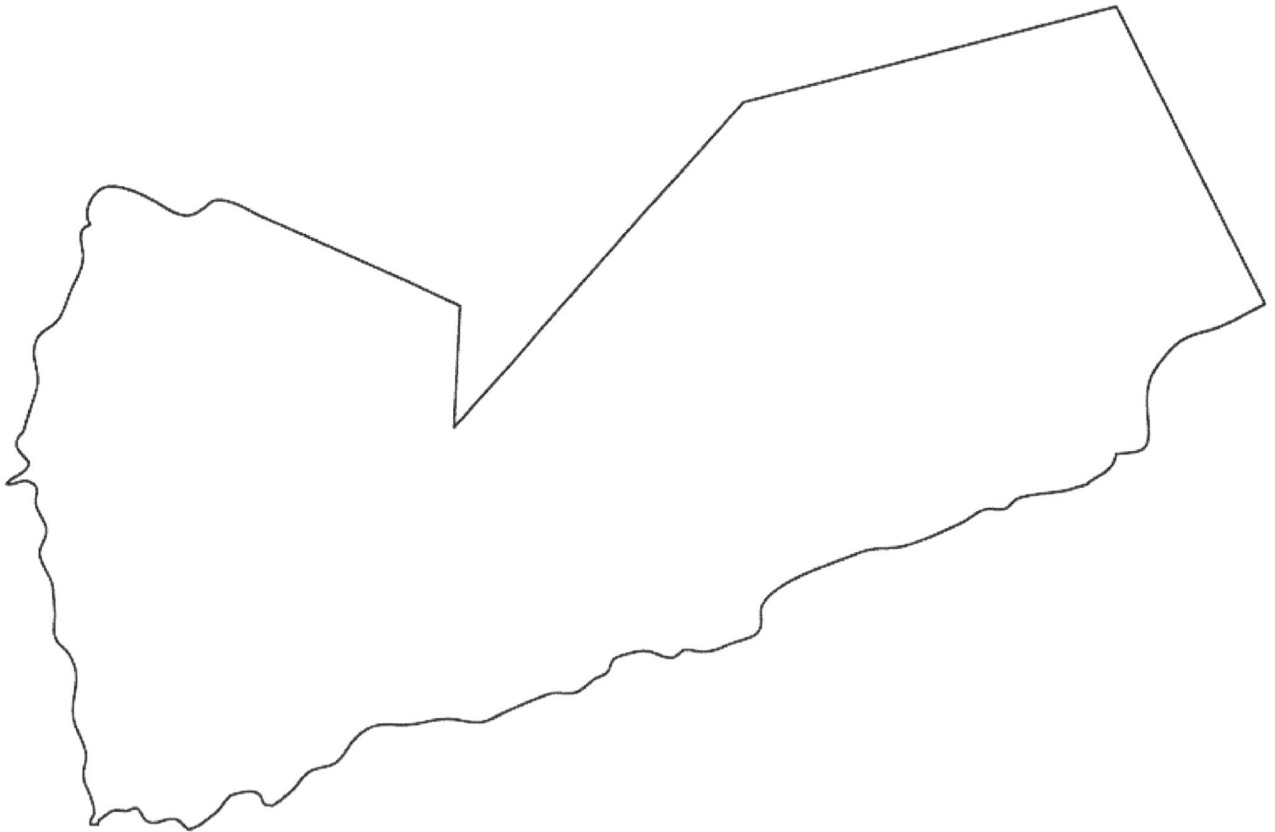

Label the capital city and any major physical features such as mountains, rivers, oceans or seas **in or around** this country.

Country Name: Yemen

FACTS

Population:_____

Area: _____

Type of Government: _____

Capital City: _____

Religion(s): _____

Language(s): _____

Currency: _____

Climate: _____

Time Zone: _____

Major Exports

1:_____

2: _____

3: _____

Mountains, Rivers and Lakes

1:_____

2: _____

3: _____

Other Cool Things about this Country

1:_____

2: _____

3: _____

4: _____

About Exploring
Expression

My name is Brandy Champeau

I am an author, speaker and curriculum developer. Through my company, Exploring Expression, I help parents, caregivers and educators of K12 students become the very best expression of themselves so that they can make learning fun, easy and natural not just for their children, but for themselves as well.

At Exploring Expression, we focus on 4 specific offerings:

1. We build quality learning resources for K12 students
2. We create resources for parents and educators to help them become the best expressions of themselves and equip them to better facilitate learning opportunities for their children
3. We utilize public speaking platforms to spread the message of becoming the best expression of yourself through the cultivation of a learning lifestyle
4. We help people with a message find their voice, publish their books and create curriculum or training to share with the world

As you can see, our passion is learning - learning about yourself and learning about the world. We focus on self-improvement and education. Because in the end it all comes down to learning. Learning doesn't have to be hard and it doesn't have to be boring. At Exploring Expression we want to help you put the engagement and excitement back into education and to put the education back into life.

CONNECT WITH US

We would love to hear from you!

https://ExploringExpression.com

ExploringExpression@gmail.com

https://www.facebook.com/ExploringExpression

https://www.Instagram.com/ExploringExpression

https://www.twitter.com/ExExAdmin

http://www.Pinterest.com/ExploringExpression

https://bit.ly/2KZrSFG

Collect all 5 Geography Factbooks!!

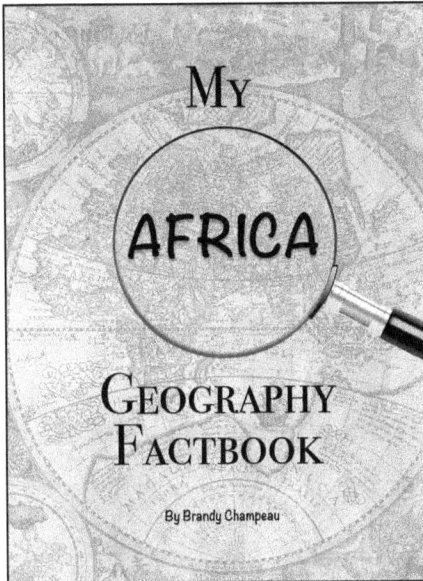

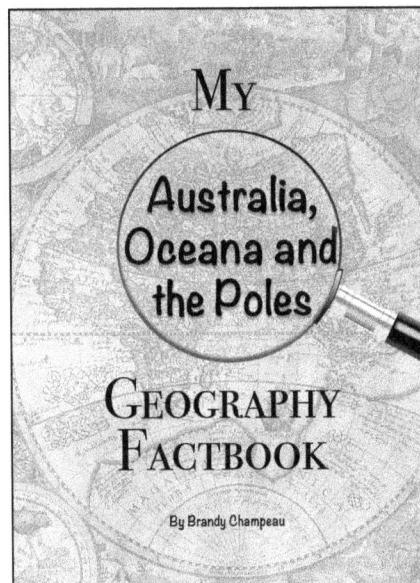

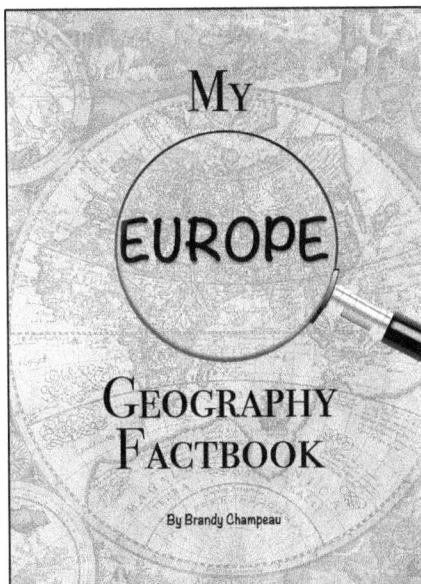

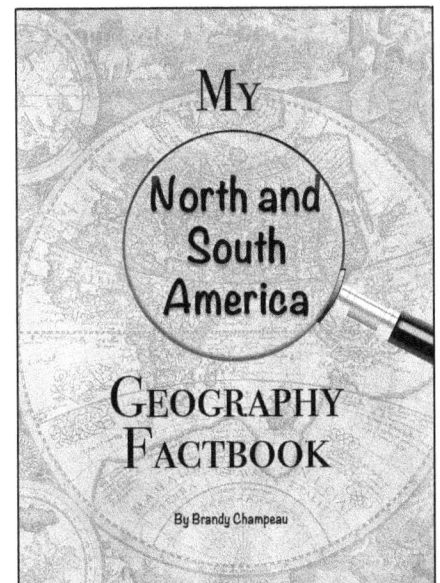

My

AFRICA

GEOGRAPHY
FACTBOOK

By Brandy Champeau

My

Australia, Oceana and the Poles

GEOGRAPHY
FACTBOOK

By Brandy Champeau

My

ASIA

GEOGRAPHY
FACTBOOK

By Brandy Champeau

My

EUROPE

GEOGRAPHY
FACTBOOK

By Brandy Champeau

My

North and South America

GEOGRAPHY
FACTBOOK

By Brandy Champeau

Available Now at https://ExploringExpression.com or on
Amazon!!

Introducing Celebrating Today

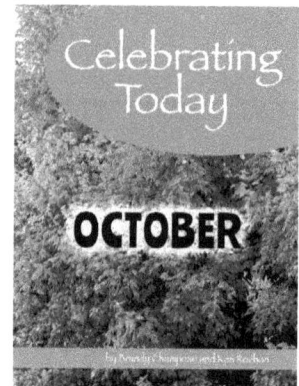

Celebrating Today
AUGUST

Celebrating Today
SEPTEMBER

Celebrating Today
OCTOBER

These books are half journal, half information, and all fun.

Everyday is worth celebrating. It doesn't matter if it is a bad day, a good day or a boring day. It's still worth celebrating simply because you still have today. Every day is a new opportunity for greatness and living your best expression.

So Let's start celebrating - Today!

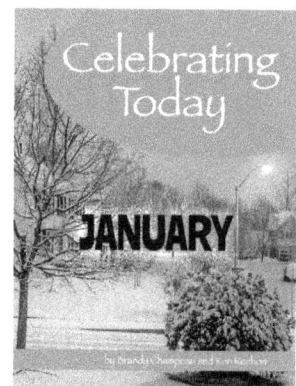

Celebrating Today
NOVEMBER

Celebrating Today
DECEMBER

Celebrating Today
JANUARY

Available Now at https://ExploringExpression.com or on Amazon!!

Also by Brandy Champeau

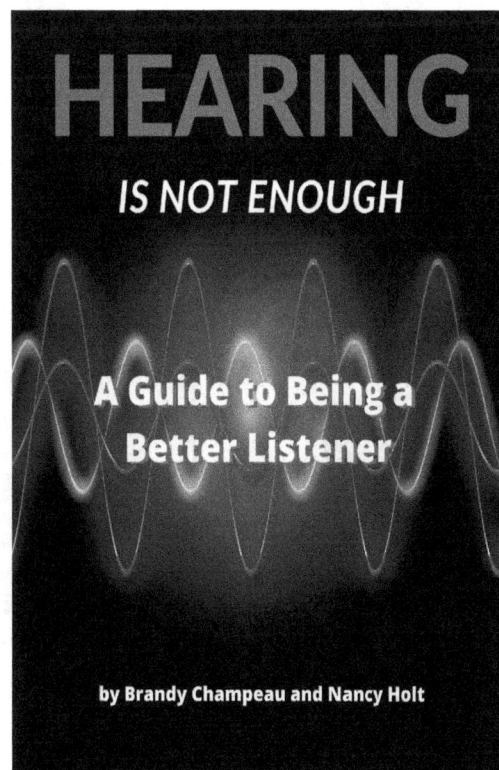

100 THINGS I DIDN'T KNOW BEFORE
MY LEARNING JOURNAL

90 Days To Your Better Expression
A Journal Experience
Brandy Champeau

HEARING
IS NOT ENOUGH
A Guide to Being a Better Listener
by Brandy Champeau and Nancy Holt

Check out these Children's Books and Workbooks by Brandy Champeau.

Available at ExploringExpression.com or on Amazon

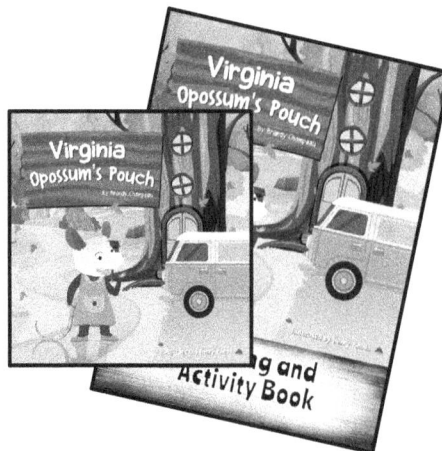

www.ingramcontent.com/pod-product-compliance
Lightning Source LLC
Chambersburg PA
CBHW080334270326
41927CB00014B/3213

9 781954 057036